The Works of Richard Greenham Volume 1
with chapters by C. Matthew McMahon

Copyright Information

The Works of Richard Greenham Volume 1, by Richard Greenham, with chapters by C. Matthew McMahon Edited by Therese B. McMahon

© 2023 by Puritan Publications and A Puritan's Mind

Published by Puritan Publications
A Ministry of A Puritan's Mind®
Crossville, TN: Puritan Publications, 2023
www.puritanpublications.com
www.apuritansmind.com

All rights reserved. No part of this publication may be reproduced, stored in a retrieval system or transmitted in any form by any means, electronic, mechanical, photocopy, recording or otherwise, without the prior permission of the publisher, except as provided by USA copyright law.

First Electronic Edition 2023
First Modern Print Edition 2023
Manufactured in the United States of America

eISBN: 978-1-62663-469-5
ISBN: 978-1-62663-470-1

Table of Contents

Meet Richard Greenham 5

The Christian Walk 12

A Treatise of Blessedness 17

Directions for Reading and Understanding the Scriptures 27

The First Treatise for An Afflicted Conscience 40

The Second Treatise for An Afflicted Conscience 83

The Marks of a Righteous Man 96

Sure Signs of Election for Those Who Have Been Brought Low 105

A Treatise on Self-Examination Before and After the Lord's Supper 108

A Treatise on the Fear of God 124

A Treatise on the Resurrection 138

A Treatise on Hypocrisy 157

A Treatise on Anger 165

A Treatise on the Doctrine of Fasting 172

Notes on Our Salvation 179

Table of Contents

The Sending of the Holy Spirit 182

A Brief Treatise on Prayer 229

Directions for Consolation 242

A Set of Wholesome Guidelines or Directions for a Christian Life 247

APPENDIX: A Marriage Contract 250

Other Works Published by Puritan Publications . 259

Meet Richard Greenham

By C. Matthew McMahon, Ph.D., Th.D.

Richard Greenham, A.M. (1531-1594) was a most excellent servant of Christ, born about the year 1531, and educated in Pembroke hall, Cambridge. There he earned his degrees in arts, and was chosen as a fellow. On his removal from the university, he became pastor to the congregation at Drayton, near Cambridge; where he continued many years, not sparing himself to promote the salvation of souls. He was a hard student, and constantly rose, winter and summer, at four o'clock in the morning. He always preached twice on the Lord's Day, and catechized the young people of his church. He usually preached four times and catechized once, during the week; and for the greater convenience of his people, where these week-day services were observed early in the morning.

He was a man of uncommon zeal, and was so remarkably passionate in his preaching, that at the conclusion of the service, his perspiration was so great, that his shirt was usually as wet as if it had been drenched in water. He was more concerned to be useful, than to obtain any worldly reward. Therefore, he refused several lucrative vocational offers.

He naturally cared for souls, and manifested on all occasions a warm concern for their salvation. At the same time, he was not unmindful of their temporal comfort, but abounded in acts of liberality to the poor and distressed; for which he and his family often suffered need.

In addition to his public ministerial labors, he had a remarkable talent for comforting afflicted consciences; and in this department the Lord greatly blessed his endeavors. Having himself waded through the deep waters, and labored under many painful conflicts, he was eminently qualified for relieving others. The fame of his usefulness in resolving the doubts of inquiring souls, having spread through the country, multitudes from all quarters, flocked to him as to a wise physician, and by the blessing of God, obtained the desired comfort. Numerous people, who to his own knowledge had labored under the most difficult terrors of conscience, were restored to joy and peace in believing. When any complained of blasphemous thoughts, his advice was "do not fear them, but abhor them."[1]

Mr. Greenham was a man remarkable for peace. He was celebrated for promoting peace among those who were at variance, and in laboring incessantly for the peace of the church of God. He was a most exact and conscientious nonconformist, choosing on all occasions to suffer, rather than sacrifice a good conscience. Though he cautiously avoided speaking against conformity, or those things which to him appeared objectionable in the established church; lest he should give the least offence, he was suspended from his ministry, for refusing to subscribe and wear the habits. He was of the opinion that rites and ceremonies introduced into the church of Christ, without the warrant of scripture,

---

[1] Clark's *Lives* annexed to his *Martyrologie*, p. 12–14.

were of no real advantage, but productive of much superstition.[2] Therefore, he prayed that all such things, as hinderances to the success of the gospel, might be taken away. To subscribe to anything besides the word of God, or not collected from that sacred volume, he dared not do, but peremptorily refused.[3]

Whoever will read his letter to Dr. Cox, bishop of Ely, will easily perceive what manner of spirit they were of, who could bear hard upon so excellent and peaceable a divine. When he was called before the bishop, on a complaint of his nonconformity, he discovered at once, his prudence, peaceableness, and good sense. His lordship observing that there was a great schism in the church, asked him whether the blame was attached to the conformists, or nonconformists. To which Mr. Greenham immediately replied, "that it might be attached to either, or to neither. For," said he, "if both parties loved each other as they ought, and did acts of kindness for each other, thereby maintaining love and concord, the blame would be on neither side; but no matter which party made the rent, the charge of schism belonged to them." The bishop is said to have been so well satisfied with this answer, that he dismissed him in peace.[4] Mr. Greenham united with his brethren in subscribing the "Book of Discipline."[5]

---

[2] Greenham's *Works*, p. 278. Edit. 1601.
[3] *Parte of a Register*, pp. 88-89.
[4] Clark's *Lives*, p. 13.
[5] Neal's *Puritans*, vol. i. p. 423.

This worthy divine having labored in the ministry at Drayton about twenty-one years, moved to London, and became minister at Christ-church, where, in about two years, he finished his labor's. He died a most comfortable and happy death, in the year 1591, aged sixty years. Fuller, who says he died of the plague, observes, that he was an avowed enemy to nonresidents, and wondered how such men could find any comfort in their wealth. "For," he used to say, "they must see written upon all they have, this is the price of blood," Our author adds, that he was most precise in his conversation, a strict observer of the Lord's Day, and that no book made a greater impression upon the minds of the people, than his "Treatise on the Sabbath," which greatly promoted the observance of it through the nation. Mr. Strype describes him as a pious minister, but not well affected to the orders of the established church.[6]

Mr. Greenham was an excellent writer, for the time in which he lived. His works, including sermons, treatises, and a commentary on Psalm 119, which all came forth at different times, but were collected and published in one volume folio, in 1601. The excellent Bishop Wilkins speaks in high commendation of his sermons, classing them with the most valuable in his day. And his commentary, says Dr. Williams, is admirable, for the time in which it was written, both for style and method; and, like all the productions of this author, is full of spiritual unction.[7]

---

[6] Strype's *Aylmer*, p. 152.
[7] *Christian Preacher*, p. 431.

The above edition of Mr. Greenham's works was published by Mr. Henry Holland, and dedicated to the Countess of Cumberland and the Countess Dowager of Huntington. In this dedication, it is observed as follows:

> "I come as in the name of the faithful servant of Christ, Mr. Richard Greenham, a man well known unto your honors, and to those most religious patrons of all piety and good learning, the Right Honorable Earls of Huntington, Warwick, and Bedford, of blessed memory, which now sleep in the Lord. Of them was he much reverenced in his lifetime; of your honors much lamented after death; for you know the loss of such to be no small rack unto the church and people of God. Such experience and good liking have your honors had of this man of God, of his godliness and gravity, and of the manifold gifts of God in him, that I need say no more, as any way doubting of your honorable acceptation."

In the edition of his works, published in 1612, there is a dedication by Mr. Stephen Egerton,[8] another excellent puritan, to Sir Marmaduke Darrell and Sir Thomas Bloother, both knights, part of which is as follows: "Surely, if one heathen man could gather gold out of the writings of another, how much more may we, being Christians, gather not gold only, but pearls and precious stones out of the

---

[8] Puritan Publications has published Egerton's work on hearing the Scriptures, which is outstanding.

religious and holy labors of Mr. Richard Greenham, being a most godly brother; yea, more than a brother, even a most wonderful pastor, zealous preacher, and reverend father in the church of God; of whom I am persuaded that for practical divinity he was inferior to few or none in his time."

This pious divine had a strong and an unceasing attachment to the house of God. He used to say that minister's ought to frequent those places most where God has made them most useful. Having once found the sweetness of gaining souls, there should they be most desirous to resort. He had so conscientious a regard for the ordinance of public worship, that, however weak might be the talents of the preacher, he constantly esteemed it his duty, as well as his happiness, to go to the house of the Lord.

Some of His works:
Grave Councils and Godly Observations
Seven Godly and Fruitful Sermons
Meditations on Proverbs 4
Meditations on Proverbs 14
Sweet Comfort for an Afflicted Conscience
The Marks of a Righteous Man
Sweet and Sure Signs of Election
A Contract Before Marriage
Notes of Our Salvation
Of the Sabbath
A Profitable Treatise on the Reading and Understanding the Scriptures
A Short Form of Catechizing

For further study:

Fuller's Church Hist. of Britain, 1655, ix. 219; Clarke's Lives of Thirty-two English Divines (at the end of a General Martyrologie), 1677, pp. 12 sq., 169 sq.; Brook's Lives of the Puritans, 1813, i. 415 sq.; Neal's Hist: of the Puritans, 1822, i. 281, 387; Strype's Aylmer, 1821, p. 100; Whitgift, 1822, p. 6; Annals, 1824, ii. (2) 415, 417, iii. (1) 720, iv. 607; Waddington's John Penry, 1854, p. 123; Marsden's Hist. of the Early Puritans, 1860, p. 248; Cooper's Athenæ Cantabr. 1861, ii. 103, 143 sq., 356, 546; Notes and Queries, 6th ser. vii. 366, viii. 55.

The Christian Walk

By C. Matthew McMahon Ph.D., Th.D.

The core of theology, as historically and biblically understood, revolves around *living for God (i.e. doing all things for his glory as he does)*. William Ames articulated *theology* as the "doctrine or teaching of living to God." This was further refined by Peter van Mastricht, who said, "Theology is doctrine or teaching of living to God through Christ." Add into this, by the power of the Spirit and you have a formula for success; living for God through Christ, empowered by the act of walking in the Spirit.

The Apostle Paul emphasized that if believers live in the Spirit, they should also *walk* in the Spirit (Gal. 5:25). This "walk" is not a mere stroll but an orderly march, akin to a military term. As soldiers of Christ, believers are given marching orders. If they genuinely live in the Spirit, they should *walk* in the Spirit, engaging in spiritual battles daily on behalf of King Jesus for his glory and their good. This spiritual walk contrasts with the works of the flesh and signifies a deep discipleship, where believers are led by Christ through the Spirit to mirror his character and actions.

This spiritual march stands in contrast to the pitfalls of pride, as highlighted in Galatians 5:26, "Let us not be desirous of vain glory, provoking one another, envying one another." Instead of yielding to these temptations, Christians are called to walk in the Spirit, putting to death the deeds of the flesh and fostering unity.

The Bible is rich with references to *walking* with God. From Adam's early days in the Garden of Eden, where "they heard the sound of the LORD God walking in the garden in the cool of the day," (Gen. 3:8), to figures like Enoch who "walked with God three hundred years," (Gen. 5:22) and Noah who "walked with God," (Gen. 6:9), walking with God has been synonymous with a saving relationship with Him. This relationship was disrupted and destroyed by sin, as seen when Adam and Eve *hid* from God after the Fall. They *ran* and hid.

Throughout history, God's covenant promises have been intertwined with the act of *walking* with Him through Christ in the power of the Spirit. The Old Testament is filled with directives and examples of this kind of walking with God. Abraham was commanded, "I am Almighty God; walk before Me and be blameless," (Gen. 17:1). God's blessings and curses were often tied to whether his people walked in his ways or strayed from them, (as seen in passages like Lev. 26:3-4 and Lev. 26:21).

The New Testament continues this theme, emphasizing walking in the Spirit as a Christian duty. Those who walk contrary to God walk in darkness, but those who walk in Christ's truth walk in the light, as Jesus said, "I am the light of the world. He who follows Me shall not walk in darkness, but have the light of life,"

(John 8:12). Walking with God is done by faith, as Paul states, "For we walk by faith, not by sight," (2 Cor. 5:7). It's about walking in love, as Christ loved us, "Therefore be imitators of God as dear children. And walk in love, as Christ also has loved us and given Himself for us, an offering and a sacrifice to God for a sweet-smelling aroma," (Eph. 5:1-2).

Walking, in this sense, is more than just motion; it's a forward spiritual progression. I believe Christians often *miss* this. When applied spiritually, walking in the Spirit means moving closer to Jesus Christ by grace *day by day*. It's *discernable*. Christians often have little to no *sensibilities* in this.

It's essential to clarify the role of good works in this walk. Good works are evidence of salvation but not its cause. *Christ's* works are the foundation of salvation. Good works by believers demonstrate that they *have been* saved by Christ. In essence, while faith alone justifies, the faith that justifies is *never* alone. It's always accompanied by good works, which are the fruits and evidence of genuine faith.

Why all this talk about *walking*? Richard Greenham's works are always about the way Christians *ought* to walk in the sight of God. If they want to be blessed, they walk in this way. If they want to understand how to study the Bible, they walk in this way. If they want to have the marks of a righteous man, they walk in this way. If they are to avoid hypocrisy and sinful anger, they walk in this way. In other words, Greenham is a *practical* puritan, and all his works tend to making Christians better Christians through glorifying the Lord Jesus Christ in *walking* with God by the Spirit instead of against him.

Greenham stands as a light of spiritual resilience and unwavering faith as an early puritan. Early puritans, to me, are trail blazers. It is amazing that their insight and biblical prowess is so sharp. Greenham was committed to the teachings of Christ, looking to spiritually uplift the church being both practical and biblical. His wise experience in practical theology, as depicted in this volume, offer readers a thoughtful understanding of faith, holiness, and the eternal struggle between pleasing Christ, or sinning against him.

Greenham's works are hardly academic, though that sits in the background of his studies; they are filled with a pastoral spirit, and his own personal testament shines through. Despite the hardships he faced, including the possible illness of dying of the plague and the ever-looming specter of death, his spirit remained unbroken to serve Christ in walking righteously. His own example of strength serves as a light of hope for all who seek solace and meaning in a fallen, wicked and depraved world by holding to God's directives and walk as Christ walked.

This spiritual legacy, immortalized in his works, will continue to inspire and guide sincere souls closer to Christ; *at least for those who will listen.* Like precious ointments, his biblical teachings refresh and rejuvenate, offering solace to those grappling with walking in the Christian life and the challenges they face. As we read Greenham's writings, we are reminded of the eternal nature of the soul and the fleeting nature of that which is temporary; to look to eternity and Christ there seated at the right hand of power, and to walk there with him hand in hand. Through his words, we are encouraged to remain steadfast in our faith, drawing strength from the knowledge that, in the face of adversity, with godly dedication, it will always go well the closer we are to Jesus Christ.

In Christ's immeasurable grace,
C. Matthew McMahon, Ph.D., Th.D.
John 5:39, "...search the Scriptures..."
www.apuritansmind.com
www.puritanpublications.com
www.gracechapeltn.com
From my study, September, 2023.

A Treatise of Blessedness

"Then shall the King say unto them on his right hand, Come, ye blessed of my Father, inherit the kingdom prepared for you from the foundation of the world," (Matt. 25:34).

He may be said to have tasted true blessedness, whom the Lord before all beginnings has *chosen* to salvation; whose salvation *purposed* by God the Father, is *performed* by God the Son. To whom the election by God the Father, and redemption by God the Son is *ratified* by God the Holy Spirit. In whom this assurance of faith is fashioned by the word preached. Faith breeding peace of mind; this peace causes joy, joy being accompanied with security, security working in love, love laboring with a care to please God, with a fear to displease God. From this comes a desire of well-doing to others, endeavoring to bring them to the peace with God and man, which he tastes of himself.

He is truly blessed, who besides all the former things, knows how to use prosperity moderately, and adversity patiently, waiting and looking for the accomplishment of God, his promise in the kingdom of heaven. More particularly we will entreat of true happiness by its causes and effects.

The original cause is the love of God, in ordaining us to be heirs of life eternal, (Eph. 1:4; Matt. 25:34). In which is laid open the bountiful riches of the mercy of God to us, in that before the foundation of the world was laid, the foundation of our salvation was made. Before we sinned, the remedy against sin was found. Before the malady, the Lord had prepared a medicine; before we were damned, he had purposed a way how we should be saved. In respect of this, seeing we are rather to rejoice in this, that our names are written in heaven, than if we had power (without hurt) to tread on scorpions, or had spirits subdued to us, (Luke 10:19-20), we conclude with the Prophet, Psalm 65:4, "Blessed is the man O God whom thou choosest, and causest to approach unto thee."

The substance of this blessedness is our redemption *in* Christ Jesus, which is the Lamb of God, that "taketh away the sins of the world," (John 1:29), by whose blood we have the forgiveness of our sins, (Eph. 1:7), and by whose Spirit (when we have believed the Gospel) we have the earnest of our inheritance, (Eph. 4:14). The excellent price of this is set out to us in it, in that being filthy in the blood of our sins, he washed us with his own blood, (Heb. 9:14), in that he being just, suffered for us being unjust, (1 Peter 3:18), in that we being of no strength and ungodly, he died for us, (Rom. 5:6). That while we were enemies through sin, were reconciled by him to God the Father, (Rom. 5:12). In this, seeing he is blessed whose wickedness is forgiven, and whose sin is covered, (Psalm 32:2), let not the wise man glory in his wisdom, as though it made him happy, nor the strong man glory in his strength, neither let the rich man glory in his riches, but let him that glories glory in this, that he knows the mercy of the Lord, in which consists our salvation, (Jer. 9:23-24). And let us all learn the meaning of the salutation of Elizabeth to the virgin Mary, Luke 1:42, "Blessed art thou among women, and blessed is the fruit of thy womb." In other words, you are blessed because the fruit of thy womb is blessed.

The formal cause is the illumination of God his Spirit, making us capable of the former mysteries, sealing them to us with such assurance in our hearts, that we dare boldly cry *Abba Father*, that we dare boldly say, "If God is on our side, who can stand against us?" Such blindness, folly, and incredulity naturally possesses us, that of ourselves we can neither see into these mysteries of our salvation, nor believe the thing we see concerning our comfort until we have received of this Spirit, which comes from above. For *no one* comes to Christ, unless the Father draw him; and how does he draw them but by enlightening the hearts of his elect by the Holy Spirit (John 6:44)? So, seeing these things are not revealed to us but by the Spirit, (1 Cor. 2:14), we see that blessing of the Lord Jesus to Peter, Matt. 16:17, "Blessed art thou Simon, thou Son of Jonah: for flesh and blood hath not opened this unto thee, but my Father which is in heaven."

The instrumental cause is partly within us, as faith, and partly without us, as the word, and the accessories accompanying the same, as prayer, the sacraments, and the discipline of the church. Faith being the ground of things which are hoped for, and the evidence of things which are not seen (Heb. 11:1). This so applies the promises of God to our proper and peculiar comforts, that it seals us up to the Lord, affording a certain testimony to our hearts, that we have not in vain received of the good spirit of God. Now, because there is a certain kind of faith, which Satan himself teaches in his school, and propounds as a principle to all his scholars; seeing the Papists urge faith in their unwritten truths, and the Familists will have it in their foolish revelations. The Muslims require it in their dry speculations of Mahomet, and the witch will seem to demand it in their devilish incantations, we must not believe every spirit, but trust *only* to the word of God. This is our sure loadstar and touch-stone, and being itself firm, makes our faith in it most firm, sure and unchangeable. This blessedness to have the Lord communicate himself to us by his word, is privileged above that praise, which the woman gave our Savior Christ, (Luke 11:27), as may appear by his sharp answer, "Yea blessed are they that hear the word of God and keep it." We conclude then with the Psalmist, blessed are they that dwell in the house of the Lord, they will ever praise him. Blessed is the man whose strength is in the Lord, and in whose heart are his ways, (Psalm 84:4-5). If the Queen of Sheba counted those men happy, that might stand before Solomon, and hear his wisdom, (2. Chron. 9:7), if David thought it a high recompence and prince-like benefit to prefer the son of Barzillai to sit at the table of Solomon, how great is our happiness to hear the wisdom of Christ? How high is our blessedness to sit at the table of the Lord, if not Solomon, but a greater than Solomon is present; where not Solomon, but a wiser than Solomon speaks to us? Behold then the causes of true blessedness, which are our election, redemption, illumination, and sanctification. All these are sealed to us by the Holy Spirit, the Spirit working faith through the word preached, Christ Jesus so sending his Spirit to renew us. God the Father sending his Son to redeem us, redeeming us to call us, calling us to justify us, justifying us to sanctify us, sanctifying us he seals us by his Spirit. And so, by all these he lays the sure groundwork of our salvation and eternal blessedness.

Concerning the *effects* of blessedness, some are inward and some are outward; the effects inward are partly in respect of ourselves only, and partly in regard both of ourselves and of others. Those in ourselves are either concerning mortification, or about our sanctification. The first of these is both truly and orderly couched in that sermon of the Lord Jesus, Matt. 5, where those men are set in the first rank who are emptied both of the opinion of their own wisdom, and of all persuasion of their own righteousness. And of these it is said, "Blessed are the poor in spirit, for theirs is the kingdom of heaven." Now because many have lost their hold in judgement, who have not so thoroughly given over in affection, in the next degree happiness is promised to such, who are so far descended into the sight of their own vileness and sense of their natural corruptions, that they are not only convinced of an unrighteousness inherent in their judgements, but also are much humbled for it in their affections, of whom the Lord of comfort has in this way determined, "Blessed are they that mourn, for they shall be comforted."

Further, for that Satan labors and prevails much in overcoming exercised minds with petty shames (a thing often part of afflicted consciences) the next beatitude is allotted to them, that are *meek* in spirit, who mourn rather in themselves, possessing their souls in patience, than murmur against others, as laboring in a secret disdain of them. And of this sort of mourners the Lord Jesus has pronounced this judgement, "Blessed are the meek, for they shall inherit the earth." Neither must we be of too abject a spirit, as they that will patiently suffer all things, because they would be troubled with nothing , for that would be more akin to a Stoic (as unchristian), than a heroic and Christian meekness. But willingly submitting our necks to the yoke, by the Lord's appointment imposed upon us, we are rather patiently to wait for the time of our deliverance, and by laboring to keep a good conscience, we are to *hunger and thirst after righteousness*. Here with the credit of the Lord's own word, we shall in his good time be satisfied.

Now that we may continue sanctification with mortification, as we join together Christ's passion and resurrection, let us add something of those quickening graces of the Spirit, in which some effects of blessedness appear most evidently. The first is peace of conscience and joy in the Holy Spirit, (Rom. 5:2). By this we find both truce with God, and are at league with his creatures. So as both, for our comfort in the promises of God we have access to him, to rejoice under the hope of his glory. And for our confidence in the promises of God, we can lie down and sleep in many perils, because God has either means to deliver us out of them, or else is ready to sustain us in them, Psalm 3:6 and 4:8. Of this in this way speaks the Prophet, "Blessed is the people that can rejoice in thee, they shall walk in the light of thy countenance, O Lord," (Psalm 89:13). Now, lest we should deceive ourselves with some false peace and alluding joy, we put to this peace of mind sincerity, which the Holy Spirit has linked together, Psalm 32:2, "Blessed is the man to whom the Lord imputeth not iniquity, and in whose spirit there is no guile." And Psalm 119:1, "Blessed are the undefiled in the way, who walk in the law of the LORD." Beware, lest this uprightness of mind be rowdy, and void of love, without which all is as nothing but a swelling pride. So, with this we make known our faith by fruits, and our feeling by sweet effects. For love is careful to please God, and fearful to displease him. "Blessed is the man that feareth always," (Prov. 28:14). "Blessed is the man that feareth the Lord and walketh in his ways," (Psalm 128:1).

Lastly, this fear is joined with a care to please God in the obedience of his word, (Luke 11). Blessed are they that *hear the word of God and keep it*. Those effects, which concern not only ourselves but others, are of two sorts, and comprehended in Matthew 5. The first, a Christian care to work in others a taste of that sweet reconciliation, which is from God to man, or from man to man, of which it is said, Matt. 5:9, "Blessed are the peace-makers, for they shall be called the children of God." Many may undertake this duty, but on some sinister affection. Therefore, we require a feeling of the evils of others, mourning both for their inward defects and outward necessities, of whom Christ has said, "Blessed are the merciful, for they shall obtain mercy." Of the other the Psalmist speaks, Psalm 40:2, "Blessed is he that judgeth wisely of the poor," *etc*. And when wisdom joined with compassion and pity, mixed with policy, works such a moderation in our affections, as that we may use such a merciful severity, where it is needful, and a severe lenity, where the matter so requires it, this causes us to avoid on the one side taking of offence; for, "Blessed are they," the Lord Jesus says, "that are not offended at me." And on the other hand teaches us to reach out our hand to the needy. For it is a blessed thing to give rather than to receive, (Acts 20:35). The outward effects are prosperity, as a sign of God's love; and adversity as a thing sanctified to us in the cross of Christ, (Psalm 128). Many temporal blessings are propounded, not universally, but as restrained to them that fear the

Lord, because indeed they have the surest interest in them and right to them. The same happiness falls out, Psalm 144, to such as have God for their Lord. And much more is, a certain gain of happiness arises even out of the bitterness of affliction, to them that fear God, in that by this the Lord strips them from some sin, with which they might have rotted. Or he sharpens them up to some actions of godliness, in which their zeal began to freeze; or to *try* their faith, which otherwise would have been dross; or for the good of others that might make their profit by it. The Prophet's testimony of this is Psalm 99:12, "Blessed is the man whom thou chastisest, O Lord, and teachest him in thy law." To this, it may be joined that beatitude of the Lord of all blessings, Matt. 5:10, "Blessed are they that suffer persecution for righteousness sake, for theirs is the kingdom of heaven."

To draw at last to the consummation of all this, we make the full heap of all happiness after this life to be *filled* with the Lord of life, and with the sweetness of his presence, who is happy above all, that can be thought and counted happy. This is foreshowed, Matt. 25, "Come ye blessed of my Father, possess the kingdom prepared for you." And Rev. 14, "Blessed are they that die in the Lord," *etc.* For in this way shall we be joined to God the Father, the Son, and the Holy Spirit, then shall all tears be wiped from our eyes, then shall our infirmities be taken from us, then shall we dwell with the angels, and with all the hosts of heaven in most happiness, and blessedness itself.

We see now that this chain is not forged by our own mind, but framed out of God's his word, that he is indeed blessed: whom God chooses, whom Christ redeems, whom the Spirit renews, whom faith stays, whom the Word, prayer, sacraments, and discipline build up in the Lord, in whom faith breeds peace, peace sincerity, sincerity love, love a fear of displeasing, and a care of pleasing God. In whom this care strives to a mortification in poverty of mind, this poverty coming from a mourning heart, possessed in a meek spirit, which hungers after righteousness. All these things being joined with that sanctification which laments the sin of others, and relieves the needs of others, knowing to use prosperity and adversity as pledges of God's favor, and undoubtingly looking for the kingdom of heaven in the life to come. If any of these links are missing, the chain is broken. If any of these members are lacking, the body of blessedness is imperfect.

FINIS.

Directions for Reading and Understanding the Scriptures

Those things which God has joined together, no man may separate. God joined together preaching and reading of the holy Scriptures in the work of our salvation, and these may not be severed asunder. A prerequisite for both preachers of God's Word and masters of the sciences, arts, and trades is the sound learning, and then practicing, of their subject matter. We must be persuaded as to how much more necessary it is to have seasoned spiritual guides go before us in the way to salvation. Further, it must be understood that preaching is the most principal means to increase[9] and beget faith and repentance in God's people (Deut. 18:18, 33:10; Lev. 10:11; Mal. 2:6,-7; 2 Chron. 36:1; Isa. 50:5, 7, 8; 53:1, 55:10-11, 57:19, 57:19, 58:1, 61:1, 62:15; Matt. 13:3, 28:19-20; Eph. 4:11-14; Rom. 10:14-15; 1 Cor. 1:21, 1 Pet. 1:23, 25). And where this ordinary means of salvation fails, the people for the most part perish (Prov. 29:18, Hos. 4:6; 2 Chron. 15:13, Isa. 56:9; Matt. 15:14; Luke 11:52). But the reading of the Scriptures publicly in the Church of God, and privately by ourselves, is a special and ordinary means to beget and increase faith in us,[10] and it is likewise proved (Deut. 6:6, 11:18; Psa. 1:2; John 5:39; Matt. 14:15; Rom. 15:14; 2 Pet. 1:19; Neh. 8:8; Acts 13:15;

---

[9] Preaching God's ordained means of salvation.
[10] Reading of the Scriptures publicly in the church.

15:21). The manifold fruit which comes from the reading of the Scriptures proves the same.

Reading establishes the foundation for preaching, for none can be profitable hearers of preaching that have not been trained up in reading the Scriptures or hearing them read. Many disadvantages come from the neglect of reading, like the inability to know when a statement is from the Canonical Scriptures, the Apocrypha, the Scriptures themselves, or other writers. In other words, without some level of personal knowledge of the Bible, the hearer cannot discern when the preacher is speaking his own words or those of the holy text.

Additionally, reading helps men's judgments, memories, and affections, but especially it serves to confirm their faith, which may be proved by the example of the men of Berea (Acts 17:13). It serves to discern the spirits of men (1 John 4), to affirm the confession of our faith, to stop the mouths of our adversaries, and to answer the temptations of Satan and the wicked.

But because men sin, not only in their neglect of hearing and reading, but also in hearing and reading amiss, the properties of and means for reverent and faithful reading and hearing are to be established. And these eight properties or means are:
1. Diligence
2. Wisdom
3. Preparation
4. Meditation

5. Conference
6. Faith
7. Practice
8. Prayer

The first three go before reading and preaching. The next four follow them. The last must go before them, be with them, and come after them.

1. If diligence is necessary in reading human authors, then much more is it essential in reading the Scriptures. Diligence makes a rough way plain and easy, and of good taste, which otherwise is hard and unsavory. In our diligence we must keep an even course, and not be like those who upon some sudden good notion, or by reason of some good company, or by reason of some good action, or for fear of danger, etc., draw near, but only to read for a time and soon after give it up again (Prov. 2:12; Matt. 13:54).

2. With diligence must be joined wisdom, which includes wisdom in subject matter, order, and time. For lack of wisdom in the subject matter they read, many sin by studying other books before the Scriptures, and others by attempting to understand those mysteries in Scripture that are not revealed while ignoring those truths that are revealed. A biblical example is when John and James contended over who should sit at Christ's right and left hands respectively, but they overlooked the more important truths. In another example the disciples asked Christ in Acts 1:6, "Will you at this time restore the kingdom to Israel?" At the same time, they

did not ask the means to come to the kingdom of heaven, which was the more important matter. And in things revealed many will curiously and busily search for things not profitable, as genealogies, while neglecting the things that are to be searched for spiritual profit. And some ignorant about how to reform themselves will be talking of reforming the Church. Consider that if the preacher must give milk to the weak and stronger meat to the stronger Christians, should not the hearers also apply this doctrine to their own reading and their own capacities?

Wisdom is in order also. Men must be first grounded in the principal points of doctrine. We must first lay the foundation and then build upon the same. We must also keep an order in our readings, and not be now in this place, now in another. For order is the best help for memory and understanding. He that reads a little Scripture well profits more than he that reads much otherwise, just as the one who stands in the right path does better than the one who runs in the wrong direction. Therefore, for lack of order many read much but profit little.

Finally, wisdom must be used in discerning the times for reading. We must not read always and do nothing else, as some failing in one extreme are then driven by Satan to fail in the other. The Sabbath is wholly to be spent in such exercises, but on other days, only in the morning, at noon, and in the evening, when we may redeem the day from our work and our calling.

These are the three times when David and Daniel prayed, and herein is contained all the worship of God. We must do as much as we can every day, and no day must pass without it. God has made everything beautiful in his time (Eccl. 3:11).

3. Preparation follows diligence and wisdom. If a man goes away without profit, either not understanding or misunderstanding the Scripture, a lack of preparation is the cause. Preparation includes the fear of God his Majesty, faith in Jesus Christ, and a good and honest heart with an insatiable desire for God's Word.

There are many biblical accounts of God's people seeing visions. But always before God sent the vision, he put the fear of God in their heart. Why? Because it engenders teachableness and meekness of mind. This is clearly seen in Isaac, who first feared, and then said, "I have blessed Jacob, and he shall be blessed." We see it also in the woman of Samaria (John 4:7), and in the men in Acts 2. When there is a lack of reverent fear first, men dare to check and evaluate and question God's Word. But those who fear God are swift to hear and slow to speak (James 1:19). These will secure God's Word in their hearts, as did the virgin Mary when visited by the angel of God. Though they kick against the Word and spurn it, if God once touches them with his fear, then they will acknowledge it to be the blessed Word of God.

Fear can come on a man without him expecting it. But if he then goes to God, he shall find some excellent blessing, by either having his understanding enlightened or by some good affections God puts into him. This fear is in respect to God's Majesty and our own corruption, to correct the pride of reason and to control our affections. Experience will show that when our reason and affections are tamed by misery, calamity, sickness, and inward grief, then we are very teachable. And when men err, then the pride of their reason is punished, as in heretics and profane persons. Contrarily, God's good spirit rests upon the humble to clear their understandings after they crucify their understanding and affections and offer them up in a sacrifice to God.

Faith in Christ is the second thing in this preparation. We must exercise faith when we come to read, looking on him as on the Messiah that must teach us all things. He is the Lion of the tribe of Judah, to whom it is given to open the book of God. He opened the hearts of the disciples going to Emmaus. Preachers build hay and stubble when they do not preach Christ but seek credit and preferment by preaching themselves. Heretics differ among themselves, yet they all agree in this.

A heart prepared to learn is required (Prov. 17:16). Our Lord Jesus Christ said that those who brought forth fruit after hearing the Word – some thirty, some sixty, some a hundred fold, were those that received the Word with a good and honest heart (Luke 8). Men do not hear the Word to salvation because they come without a heart prepared to learn.

Next are the properties that must follow our readings: the first is meditation. Men may read or hear the Word diligently, but without meditation it bears no fruit. Meditation makes that which we have read become our own. He is blessed who meditates in God's Law day and night (Psa. 1:2). Meditation involves both the mind and understanding, and the heart and its affections.

Meditation of the understanding is when reason considers deeply those things read or heard, which the wise heathen calls the refining of judgement, the life of learning. They that lack this, regardless of how much they have heard or read, shall never have sound and settled judgment. This is one reason why it is said that the greatest clerks are not the wisest men.

Meditation of the affections is when we take what is now in our understanding and digest it and work it into our affections. It is a continual searching of ourselves, laboring to lay up God's truths in the treasures of our heart. The understanding will fade away in time unless it is joined with the heart's affections.

Mindful meditation and understanding of the Scripture must come first, but the heart must soon attach, or it will be lost altogether. We must possess sound judgment before we either fear or cheer up our hearts, lest we have false fears or false joys. Many are of sound judgment, and yet their hearts have not been purged and touched. They can give sound counsel to others, but cannot follow it themselves, because they have not joined their affection with judgment. Meditation without reading is erroneous, and reading without meditation is barren.

The next thing is conference. In natural things man stands in need of help. How much more, then, do we need help from others in spiritual things. As iron sharpens iron, so one friend sharpens another (Prov. 27). And as two eyes see more, two ears hear more, and four hands can do more. This is a special communion of saints that God has promised where two or three are gathered together in his name, that he will be present with them by his spirit as he was corporally with his disciples going to Emmaus.

Conference should be sought with ministers of God, our equals, and others. However, conference with our equals must be of those things which we heard from our ministers, as it must be kept also in meditation, which is a conference with ourselves. We must for a time be like hungry babes before our ministers because we cannot run before we walk. So, we cannot go forward without a leader. No man may presume to understand that which should be understood, but labor to understand according to the measure of responsibility, as God has dealt to everyone their measure of faith. And when the foundation has been laid, then you build the walls and pillars.

The Eunuch would not attempt to understand the Scripture he was reading without a guide, but he laid it up in his heart as the Virgin Mary did. For lack of true humility, conference is slandered, because it is used after an evil manner, before being grounded in the principal points of doctrine. Secondly, we must come in love without anger, envy, or desire for victory. Therefore, in conference we must use the preparation spoken of before, otherwise there will be much wrangling and conference will come to no good.

Lastly, we must be honest before men, that it may be done wisely, without confusion and destruction. This is the difference between the conference of the godly and righteous and those of heretics.

The next means of reverent reading and hearing is faith: the Word must be mixed with faith (Heb. 4:2), as the Word profits nothing if it is not mixed with faith. But all do not have faith. This is why the prophet Isaiah said, "Lord who will believe our report?" And Luke 18:8, "when the Son of man cometh, shall he find faith on the earth?" Diligence, wisdom, preparation, meditation, and conference must all be used to refine faith, for as gold is purified seven times in the fire, so faith which is much more precious than gold, must go through all these means.

A merchant must have something to sell before he can be a merchant, but he labors to increase his means so he can get more. Likewise, we must first believe in Jesus Christ by a general faith. But then we use all the aforenamed means to increase our knowledge and faith in particulars. One may be a faithful person generally, and yet an unbeliever in particulars.

There is a difference between faith and opinion or knowledge, for our knowledge and opinions vanish away in afflictions. But as gold is tried in the fire, so faith will abide the fire of affliction. Satan winnowed Peter, but his faith did not fail, for Christ did not fail. Christ prayed for him and for all his disciples, and for all believers, that their faith should not fail.

The next property of reverent hearing and reading of the Word is practice, or a desire that the Word increase our faith and repentance. Psalm 119:98 says, "Thou through thy commandments hast made me wiser than mine enemies: for they are ever with me." The practice of infidels is nothing because it is not joined with faith. But Christ said, "Blessed are they which hear and do." And James, "faith without works is dead," which is to say that outward spiritual practice is the assurance of inner faith. He that puts his faith into practice is compared to him that builds his house upon a rock. Our works are not the foundation of the house, but rather we build upon Christ when we join the fruits of our faith with knowledge. Our works speak for us to our consciences and to others. Our Savior Christ said, "the servant who knows the will of his master and does not do it shall be beaten with many stripes: for it is worse to offend of knowledge than of ignorance."

And why should he give us more if we do not practice what we have? For to him that has, shall be given more, but from him that does not practice, what he has been given shall be taken away. The reason some either continue or increase in their blindness is because they would not practice what they knew, so that whatever they had gained is taken from them. If a good conscience is not joined with faith, faith shall be taken away and errors increase. So if we grow forgetful, we must confess that the lack of practice is the cause. The rule of reason in all things is that the best way of learning is by practice. How much more will God increase our faith and our gifts (our "talents") if we practice?

The last property is prayer, which must be used both in the beginning, in the middle, and in the end. Prayer must be in all the former means, for without it we can never use them, nor have any blessing by them. Further, contained in prayer is both prayer and thanksgiving.

Prayer must be used when we read, as in 1 Corinthians 2, "The eye has not seen, etc." meaning not only the joys contained in the kingdom of heaven, but even those that are contained in the Word. And again in the same place, "As no man knows the heart of a man but the spirit of man, so no man knows the meaning of the Lord in his Word except God give him his spirit to declare it unto him." And if we pray when we come to our meat and drink that God may give nourishment to us by them, then how much more must we pray that God will nourish us by his Word, for else we cannot profit thereby. And as no man dare touch meat and drink before he prays because he does not have rights to it before it is sanctified to him by prayer, how imprudent

Directions for Reading and Understanding the Scriptures

are they that dare touch God's book without prayer, or thinking that otherwise they are entitled to it? Paul may plant, and Apollos may water, but God gives the increase. So, if any are without spiritual understanding, though they have long heard the Word, it is because God has not revealed his will to them. Men may be diligent to read and hear the Word, yet they shall not profit by it if God does not infuse the hearing of his Word by his Spirit. And though they meditate and confer, yet they shall be punished for taking liberties with their thinking and speaking, instead of praying for God's spirit to guide them.[11]

Many rely on their knowledge but lack faith because they lack prayer. And others rest in knowledge but never practice because they do not ask God in prayer to write his law in their hearts by his Spirit, that he may accomplish his work in them. They that take anything in hand without prayer, assume in error to have power in themselves.

For thanksgiving, if we are bound to praise God when he has fed our bodies, how much more when he has fed our souls? And shall not God be justly offended with us if we do not thank him for refreshing us with physical nourishment and sleep? And shall we not tremble for fear of revenge, if we have not praised God for any light that he has put into us? For lightning is followed by darkness, and after much feeling comes deadness. By this same means Satan goes about to take

---

[11] Many rest in knowledge and lack faith ... why?

all God's graces from us. David said, "Blessed art thou Lord, O teach me thy statutes." This shows that we must always praise God before we come to read his Word. Many are fervent in asking, but slow to give thanks. Finally, if we would give thanks to God, it would ease us greatly in asking, and God would not punish us in taking his graces from us.

FINIS.

The First Treatise for An Afflicted Conscience

Proverbs 18:14 "The spirit of a man will sustain his infirmity: but a wounded spirit who can bear it?"

This Scripture is not only worthy to be engraved in steel with the pen of a diamond, and to be written in letters of gold, but also to be stored and recorded by the finger of God's spirit in the tables of our hearts. This sentence briefly tells us that whatever trouble befalls a man (his mind being undaunted), he will bear it without bias: but if a man's spirit is once troubled and dismayed, he doesn't know how to be delivered. And it's no wonder: for if the mind of man is the fountain of consolation, which offers comfort to him in all other troubles; if that becomes comfortless, what shall comfort it? If it is void of help, *how* shall it be helped? If the eye, which is the light of the body, is darkness, how great is that darkness? If the salt, which flavors all things, is tasteless, what is it good for? If the mind, which sustains all troubles, is troubled, how *intolerable* is that trouble? To show this better, I will first declare how great a punishment from God this wound of conscience is. Secondly, I will teach how this trouble of mind may be prevented and avoided. Lastly, I will lay down how God's children, falling in some measure into this affliction of spirit, may be recovered out of it.

For the first part, the severity of this malady is seen either by some proper consideration of the persons that have felt it, or by some wise comparison made between this grief of mind, and other outward griefs that befall man.

The persons in whom we may consider this wound of spirit are either merely natural men or such as are renewed by the Spirit of God. The merely natural men are either the heathens, such as never knew God in Christ, or carnal professors, such as have not professed Christianity correctly. If we look among the heathens, how many of them have willingly endured all poverty, and have been content to divest themselves of all worldly treasures? How some of them (while their minds were not dejected) have suffered imprisonment, exile, and extreme bodily torture, rather than betray their countries? How many of them have endured many injuries, and borne outward troubles with some ease and no resistance, while their minds were at liberty? And yet, if you look not into the average but the best and most excellent men among them, even their wise philosophers, eloquent orators, and skillful poets, who thought that endurance and forbearance were the highest points of virtue, you shall see when once some great distress of mind wounded them, some would end it by preparing a cup of deadly poison; some would violently and voluntarily run on the enemies' pikes; some would throw themselves from high mountains; some would not hesitate to stab their own bodies with daggers, or similar instruments of death. All of which men seemed to have great courage in bearing many harms, as long as their minds were not overcome. But when the divine and supreme Essence (which they acknowledged to be God) did by his power thwart and overthrow their cunning schemes and headstrong attempts, so that without hope of remedy they were ensnared in pensiveness and sorrow of mind. Then not being able to bear such a heavy burden, they shrank down, and by violent death would rid themselves of that unrest and impatience of their troubled minds.

But let us come closer; and whether we observe the Papists, or the Family of Love, or the common sort of Christians, we shall see they will pass quietly through many afflictions, whether because they have a spirit of slumber and numbness cast upon them, or because they have hardened themselves through some senseless dullness, as men carved out of hard oaks or sculpted out of marble stones, I do not know. But yet when the Lord shall let loose the cord of their consciences, and shall set before their faces their sins committed; see what fearful ends they have, while some of them by hanging themselves, some by casting themselves into the water, some by cutting their own throats, have rid themselves of these unbearable griefs. Now where is the difference that some die so senselessly, and some dispatch themselves so violently? Surely, the ones feeling no sin depart like brutish Swine; the others, overburdened with sin, die like barking dogs.

But let us come to the children of God, who have in some degree felt this wound of mind; and it will appear both in the members and in the head, of all burdens to be a thing most intolerable, to sustain a wounded conscience. And to begin, let us put in the first rank Job, that man of God commended to us by the Holy Ghost, as a mirror of patience: who although for his riches he was the wealthiest man in the land of Uz; for his authority, might have scared a great multitude; and for his substance, was the greatest of all the men in the East: yet when the Sabeans came violently and took away his Cattle; when the fire of God falling from heaven, burnt up his sheep and his Servants; when the Chaldeans had taken away his Camels, when a great wind knocked down his house upon his children, although indeed he tore his garments, which was not so much for impatience, as to show that he was not senseless in these evils: yet it is said that he, worshipping, blessed the Name of the Lord, saying: "Naked came I out of my mother's womb, and naked shall I return again: The Lord giveth, and the Lord taketh away, blessed be the Name of the Lord," (Job 1:21). But behold, when at the strange conversation of his comfortless friends, his mind began to be afraid, which was not so in all his former trial; when his conscience began to be troubled, when he saw the Lord fasten in him sharp arrows, and to set him up as a target to shoot at. When he thought God caused him to possess the sins of his youth. This glorious pattern of patience could not bear his grief; he was heavy, and now cannot commend the image of a wounded spirit, to all that come after. David, a man chosen according to the Lord's *own heart*; Ezekiel, a pure worshipper of God and careful restorer of true religion; Jeremiah, the Prophet of the Lord, sanctified and ordained to that office before he was formed in his mother's womb, were rare and singular in the graces and favor of God. Yet when they felt this wound, piercing them with grief of heart, they were like mourning sparrows, like chattering cranes, like pelicans casting out fearful cries, they thought themselves as in the grave, they wished to have lived solitarily, they were like bottles parched in the smoke, they were like mourning doves, unable to utter their words without sighs and groans, their hearts clung to the dust, and their tongues to the roofs of their mouths.

But above all, if these were not enough to persuade us in this doctrine, there remains one example, whom we affirm to be the perfect anatomy of an afflicted mind. This is the Lord and Savior Jesus Christ, the image of the Father, the head of the body, the mirror of all graces, the wisdom, righteousness, holiness, and redemption of all the saints, who endured the cross even from his youth upward; and in addition to poverty, lowliness, hunger, did willingly submit to the great trouble of contempt and scorn, and that among those where he should have had a rightfully deserved honor, in respect to the doctrine he taught them, and in regard to the many miracles he performed among them; such as healing the sick, giving sight to the blind, restoring life to the dead; this unkindness, however, did not affect him so deeply. But when he was established as a sacrifice for all, when he was to bear our weaknesses, and carry our sorrows, when he was afflicted and struck by God, humbled and wounded for our wrongdoings, when he would be broken for our sins, and the punishment for our peace was upon him; then he cried out, "My soul is heavy even unto death." Then he prayed, "Lord, if it be possible, let this cup pass from me." But how does he pray? With sweating; how does he sweat? With drops of blood; how long does he pray? Three times; when does his agony end? Not until he was dead; what did he say when he was ready to leave? "My God, my God, why hast thou forsaken me?" (Matthew 27:46). Was this for his human death, as some have thought? No, no, wicked men have died without complaint, whose patience then might seem to surpass his; it was his suffering in his human spirit, which encountered the wrath of God, his Godhead suppressing itself for a while; he suffered indeed many torments in body, but much more heavily did the wrath of God lie upon his soul.

If this consideration of an afflicted spirit in these examples does not sufficiently show what a grievous thing it is to bear a wounded conscience, let us proceed to compare this with other evils that affect the nature of man. There is no sickness for which medicine doesn't provide a remedy; there is no wound that surgery won't afford a salve; friendship helps poverty; there is no imprisonment from which there isn't hope for freedom; suit and favor can recover a man from banishment; authority and time wear away scorn. But what medicine cures, what surgery salves, what riches ransom, what favor helps, what authority soothes, what favor relieves a troubled conscience? All these united together in alliance (though they would conspire a confederation) cannot help this one distress of a troubled mind; and yet this one comfort of a peaceful mind does marvelously cure, and comfortably ease all other sorrows whatsoever. For if our assistance were as an army of armed soldiers; if our friends were the rulers of the earth; if our possessions were as vast as between the East and the West; if our food were as manna from heaven; if our clothing were as costly as the priestly garments of Aaron; if every day were as glorious as the day of Christ's resurrection; yet if our minds are filled with dread at the judgments of God, these things would comfort us little. Let experience speak. If a troubled mind doesn't impair health, dry up the blood, waste the marrow, wear away the flesh, consume the bones, if it doesn't make all pleasures painful, and shorten this life, certainly no wisdom can counsel it, no advice can alleviate it, no relief can cure it, no eloquence can persuade it, no power can overcome it, no authority will frighten it, no charm can harm it. And yet, on the other hand, if a man languishes in sickness, so long as his heart is whole, and is convinced of the health of his soul, his sickness does *not* distress him. If a man is scorned, but is precious in the sight of God and His angels, what loss has he? If a man is banished, but does not doubt that heaven is his country, and that he is a citizen among the saints, it does not dismay him. If a man is in trouble, but finds peace of conscience, he will quietly endure his trouble. But if the mind is troubled, who dares confront the wrath of the Lord of hosts? Who can silence the voice of despair? Who will step forward and negotiate with hell to spare us? Who dares make a pact with the devil, that he would make no claim on us? If then a good conscience helps all evils, and all other benefits in this life, in themselves, cannot help a troubled conscience; we see it is true in practice, which is here proverbially stated, "The spirit of a man will sustain his infirmity: but a wounded spirit who can bear?" (Proverbs 18:14).

Again, in all other afflictions we may have some comfort against sin; this is always accompanied by the accusation of sin. A man may be sick, scorned, impoverished, imprisoned, and banished; and yet in all these have a clear conscience; his own heart telling him that there is no particular cause for these crosses in him, but that he may endure them for the trial of his faith, or for righteousness sake and well-doing. But when the spirit is wounded, there is always guilt of sin, and when a man's spirit is troubled, he suspects all his ways, he fears all his sins, he doesn't know what sin to begin with; it creates such turmoil in him, that when it's day he wishes for night; when it's night he would have it day; his food does not nourish him, his dreams are terrifying to him, his sleep often deserts him; if he speaks, he is little eased; if he keeps silent, he seethes in unrest of heart; the light does not comfort him, the darkness terrifies him.

To continue our comparisons, all other evils are more bearable because they are temporary and pursue us only until death. But if this evil is not cured, it doesn't end in death but becomes eternal. Even the pagan men believed that death was the end of all misery, and this belief led them to end their lives and hasten their own deaths when they were in some misery. Satan convinces many to do this nowadays, ignorant of hell, which is a place of far greater pain than anything they can suffer in this world. A tormented conscience, if it had begun before, now continues, or if it was not there before, now begins and never ends for all eternity. Although sickness, poverty, imprisonment, or banishment may end in death, a wounded heart, which was temporary in this life, becomes eternal after this life. That which before death could have been healed, after death becomes incurable and unrecoverable. Therefore, it's good to consider that if the torment of conscience is so fearful in this life, how much more grievous it is to endure it in hell, where that which is infinite here is finite, where that which is measurable here is unmeasurable, where the sea of sorrow exists and this world's sorrow is but a drop; where the flame of that fire is more than just a spark in this world.

To conclude this argument: there have been some who throughout their lives have been free from all other troubles, either not feeling them at all or only in a small measure, and thus never knowing what outward trouble meant. For example, there have been men who never knew a headache for sickness, never knew what poverty meant, were never spoken evil of, always avoided the evil day of the Lord, made agreements with death, and bargains with hell; who though they could avoid any problem, they could never escape a wounded conscience, either in this life or the next. It's true that God's children can often escape it through faith and repentance, but the wicked, destined for it as their sure inheritance, are *pursued* by it the *more* they flee. If we've broken civil laws, judges may be bribed; if someone has committed a capital offense, by fleeing the country he may escape the magistrate's hands. But when our consciences tell us we've sinned against God, what bribe can we offer, or where can we flee? "Whither shall I go from thy spirit? or whither shall I flee from thy presence? If I ascend up into heaven, thou art there: if I make my bed in hell, behold, thou art there," (Psalm 139:7-8). No officer needs to summon us, no bailiff needs to fetch us, no accuser needs to testify against us; sin will arrest us, and our own conscience will accuse us, our hearts will provide evidence, and our own iniquities will declare us guilty.

We see how grievous and intolerable the burden is to have a tormented conscience, both from the experience of those who have suffered the wound of the spirit and by comparing it with other evils.

Now, let's discuss how we may prevent this and how God's children, if they fall into some degree of it (for if it becomes extreme, it's very dangerous), may safely and quietly be delivered from it. It's surprising to see many people careful to avoid other troubles, but few or none take any pains to escape the trouble of the mind, which is so grievous. People love health and loathe sickness, are moderate in diet and sleep, are skilled in medicine, and know how to avoid diseases that may cause dangerous sickness. But to avoid diseases of the soul, no one takes such pains; as if salvation and peace of mind weren't worth laboring for.

Some, ambitious for honor and unable to bear reproach, are active in every attempt to become famous and avoid civil reproach; yet to be glorious in the sight of God, they make no effort. Others, unwilling to risk legal punishment or imprisonment, will study civil law and avoid serious crimes; but when God threatens eternal punishment for breaking His commandments, no one cares for the Gospel.

And, alas, the more people seek outward pleasures and avoid inward trouble, the more they rush into it. Merchants who hope for riches may suddenly fall into despair or a hard heart. Tragic examples have shown how some, set on pleasure and not wishing to be sad, have turned their excesses into excesses of sorrow, leading to the most bitter and terrible torments of a fearful conscience.

There are others who, desiring fame, fall into vain and shameful attempts, losing not only their peace of conscience but also their reputation. The peace of conscience is a treasure beyond understanding, just as a wounded spirit is an agony indescribable except by those who have experienced it. Those who have tasted the peace of mind know its meaning, and likewise, only those who have experienced a troubled mind can *truly* speak of it.

Let us show the way that must be followed to keep us from this spiritual wound. It is similar to using medicine, both to cure diseases once we have fallen into them, and to protect us from illness before it has taken hold of us. It is the power of the Word, not only to ease the trouble of conscience when it starts to press us but also to prevent it before it has overtaken us. It's a vital aspect of worldly wisdom not to wait for medical treatment until we are deathly ill, but to be aware of God's merciful protections that defend us from it. Likewise, it's essential for a devout Christian not only to seek comfort when agony is upon him but also to use all proper aids to deal with it before it arrives. And we consider it foolish for those who won't work to keep themselves out of debt as well as pay it off when they owe it; likewise, it is madness not to be as careful to avoid all situations that may bring mental distress upon us, as we would be to find ways to escape such trouble once we've entered it.

The preventive remedies first involve searching for our sins and then examining our faith. The searching of our sins leads to the proper acknowledgment of our sins and the genuine recognition and feeling of them. The acknowledgment of our sins can be of those past, where we've sincerely repented of them, or those present, whether we're truly saddened by them.

Thirdly, it's about those hidden corruptions likely to appear during our lives, whether we fear them reverently and decide to suppress them with all our effort. Concerning past sins, we must recall those committed long ago, in our youth, middle age, or old age, so that by judging ourselves, we may not be judged by the Lord, and by accusing ourselves, Satan will not accuse us; by humbling ourselves before the Lord, He may lift us up. For many have quietly moved on, ignoring the sins of their youth, only to suddenly fall into such horror of mind that they've been overwhelmed by the violent remembrance of all their sins (John 11:35).

This examination is then proper when it reaches the mistakes of this life and the sins of our youth. Even some who have lived a righteous life and avoided gross sins have nonetheless carried the burden of their *secret* youthful sins. David prays to the Lord not to remember the sins of his youth (Psalm 25:7), and Job, the man of God, confesses that the Lord made him possess the iniquities of his youth (Job 23:6). We should not think that David or Job were notorious in wickedness in their youth; rather, they knew they were subject to youthful indiscretions, leading them to be less careful in glorifying God. This examination leads them to repent.

But it's shameful that many men, far from true repentance, boast about their youthful deeds, not only encouraging others to sin but also setting themselves against repentance. They seem to renew their old sins, finding pleasure in things that should cause shame. This also includes those who equate leaving sin with repenting for it, a fallacy against which both daily experience and the Word of God warn.

Joseph's brothers stopped their cruelty against him but didn't remember their sins with remorse until thirteen years after (Genesis 37:18-36). David abandoned his sins of murder and adultery, thinking all was well, but repented a year later, advised by the Prophet Nathan (2 Samuel 12:1-13). Many have been tormented by past sins due to a lack of true repentance.

This examination of past sins must include those committed before and after our calling to faith. We must be especially careful with those sins after knowledge, as they bite the hardest. We must examine them most specifically.

In conclusion, committing sin before knowledge is bad enough, but after receiving some enlightenment of the Spirit, sinning can breed either a hard heart or a troubled spirit. Both of these we will avoid if we truly are careful to watch over our feelings and beware that we do not fall into sin again after our deliverance.

Several men, subject to various sins, have their individual checks in their consciences: some are overcome with anger, and yet after the moody fit, they can acknowledge that "the wrath of man does not accomplish the righteousness of God," (James 1:20); some are subject to lust, and afterward, they say that it benefits them not; some are given to a continual course of vanity, who nonetheless can say that man's life has another end; some fall deeply into worldliness, and yet they are often weakened with the most terrible checks of conscience. Well, blessed are they whose hearts are truly grieved; and let them be careful who make dalliance with sin, for either hardness of heart will overtake them, or a troubled conscience will confound them. Therefore, it happens that many, spending their bodies on lust, lament that they ever abused their strength; many given too much to the pleasure of this life had grief come upon them, to remember how they have *spent* God's graces, *squandered* his good gifts, and *wasted* their time; or else, if they have not this grief, they fall into voluptuousness, and draw such thick skin upon their hearts, as will cause the strongest warnings of God's judgments to rebound, no matter how forcefully they are driven. And certainly, it is the sin of this world that men, being controlled in their consciences while praying and feeling a secret charge laid against them to be cautious of deceit in buying and selling; either have these checks diminish over time, and thus they grow to be profane; or else afterward they are greatly wounded that they have been so worldly, so eagerly pursuing earthly things, so negligently seeking heavenly things. In this way even our private thoughts (when not profited from) breed further trouble.

Now, the remedy against this trouble is willingly and knowingly *not to cherish sin*, to wish that the minister should touch on our most private and secret sins, to be glad to be privately admonished, to profit from our enemies when they reproach us; and rather to desire (in such a case) to be humbled, than to allow ourselves to be flattered. This self-examination must extend further, not only to the committing of evil but also to the omitting of good. As when (after some good action and feeling of the spirit) we begin to fight and conflict with our consciences, saying: though I must pray, I must also have time to provide for my family; if I go to hear the word of God, surely I shall risk losing this profit; if I attend the exercises of religion, I shall be cut short in the use of my pleasures. Therefore, it will be good to examine our hearts, not only in the careless not using of the means, but also in the negligent watching over the fruits of the means, saying to ourselves in this manner: I have heard a sermon, but (alas) without any feeling or impact upon my affections; I have been praying, but without the power of the Spirit; I have received the sacrament, but without those glorious and unspeakable joys that I used to taste; I saw the discipline of the

Church carried out, but without any fear of sin at all in myself, or compassion for the member censured.

And here I dare, based on my own observation, confidently affirm that outward sins have not sometimes been as grievous to God's children as that they have sometimes used the means with little reverence and even less fruit. And it's no wonder; we shall see many men at times, not so much grieved for their sickness itself, as for that they have either willingly neglected the means which might have preserved their health or that they have abused the medicine that might have restored their health. In like manner (I say), it happens with them who either irreverently have refused the means, which should keep their souls from surfeiting, or else ungratefully have abused those aids, which might have recovered them again. Therefore, it comes that some men are as much grieved for not using their good gifts to the benefit of God's Church as others are troubled for burdening the Church with unprofitable corruptions; or as we shall see a rich man sometimes as much humbled for not giving money to the poor, which he might have done, as for accumulating riches dishonestly, which he should not have done. And in this way many (having received good gifts and graces from the Lord) are seasoned and sanctified by afflictions, by which they are taught to put their gifts to use, and to offer their service to Christ, and others are forced to hide their gifts, which cannot be without some decline of God's glory, without offense to the weak, without the loss of many souls, which otherwise might be won to the Gospel, and without strengthening the hand of the adversary to slander our dark and dumb profession. All of which things will, in the end, bring terror of mind; because if the Lord cannot work upon us by taking away goods, friends, credit, wife, children, or the like, to bring us to repentance; he will surely whip our naked consciences, he will enter even into our very entrails, and pierce our secret bowels. Just as we must examine ourselves for sins of the past and present, we must use this practice in regard to future sin, and this is very necessary. For if it were so, that our life and conversation were such that neither before nor after our calling, man could justly accuse us, the hidden corruption of our nature might threaten some heinous downfall in the future, which has caused men of very good reputation and conversation to hang down their heads and fear their secret hypocrisy, as something that may break forth to the shame of all their former life, in time to come.

But because we forget to speak of those who, in examining their lives past, are much grieved for the lack of sincerity, and for private vain-glory in themselves, let us, before we go to the searching of our hearts in sin to come, speak somewhat of this. Men troubled for this private pride are either affected, or not affected. If the veil of sin was so great in them that it hid Christ from them, it is the good will of God that, by this sight of their secret sins, they should come to see the righteousness that is in Christ Jesus, and so they shall be better kept from being self-righteous Pharisees. For when, after being well brought up and leading a civil life for a long time, the devil would persuade us of some inherent righteousness in us; it is the wisdom of our God to touch us with the conscience of most hidden corruptions, and also to certify and make known to us that even from our birth there was a secret seed of sin in us, which (without the Lord watching over us) would surely have broken forth to His dishonor. As for those who have had some working in them, and yet are often plunged with severe distresses, this trouble comes to them for two specific reasons: either for some hypocrisy, that they did more in appearance than in truth, whereby the Lord brings them back again to see their corrupt actions, and that they may know all their religion to be hypocrisy, and all their righteousness to be unrighteousness; or for the abusing of their knowledge, in that they used it as a mask to cover their sin; for which God, in His providence, plunges them into misery, that they may feel what it is to abuse such a great good as the grace of God is.

To summarize, this spiritual self-examination should be used by us to *explore* our hearts, to *seek* the Lord's assistance in understanding our nature, our sins, and our salvation. It must bring us to a place of humility and repentance, reminding us of our need for Christ's righteousness. Our comfort, hope, and peace lie in our connection with Him, our Savior, who redeems and sanctifies us. We should be diligent in this practice, knowing that it is crucial to our spiritual growth and essential in our walk with the Lord.

And to return from where we digressed, to the examination of our hearts in the sin that is to come, let us observe that in God's children, there is such a jealousy that they tremble at the very first impulses, and quake at the slightest occasion of sin. However, because vice resides very close to virtue, there may sometimes be too much scrupulousness in them. This fear causes the dearest of God's saints to reason this way: *O Lord, I see how many excellent in gifts, and constant in profession for a long time, whose end did not answer their beginnings, whose deaths were not like their lives.* This is true whether we look into the word or into the world, and it is something that can humble us greatly. For though we may remember what we have been and know what we are, yet who can tell what may come to him in the future? Oh, that the serious meditation of this would dwell long upon our consciences, that with a holy jealousy we might prevent the sin that is to come.

But alas, there are some venturous knights who think it no mastery to offer themselves to masking, minstrelsy, and dancing, nor to run into quarrels, brawls, and contentions, as though they had their ears, their eyes, their hands, and their feet at their own command, to use and govern as they wish. However, God's children, better protected with His grace than those bold clownish people, are afraid of these occasions, knowing full well that their eyes may soon be provoked to lust, their ears may quickly listen to unchaste delights, their hands may suddenly strike a deadly blow, and their feet may easily be ensnared in carnal pleasures.

Beware, Oh man, be circumspect, Oh woman, that you do not prostitute yourself to too much liberty, for although in coming to such lascivious and contentious places you intended no evil, yet for your venturing without warrant, you may be over your head in sin, and plunged in some wicked attempt over your head and ears before you are aware. And because vice is so close to virtue, beware also of superstition, for still the enemy labors either to make you too bold in sin or else will cause you to be too fearful and superstitious. Either he will puff you up with presumption or assault you with desperation. To these temptations, our nature is very pliable: first to presumption, as may appear by our common speech: "hush, the preacher is but a man as I am, I am sure he has infirmities as others have; we are no angels, our nature is corrupt, we are but flesh, I am sure you would not have us be gods". In this way the devil comes to tempt; but he dresses himself in another suit when he comes to accuse, and then from a fly, he makes an elephant; from the very smallest prick of a pin, a globe of the whole earth; from a molehill, a mountain; and presses poor souls with fears and terrors that they do not know how to escape from. If he cannot bring them to make no conscience where they should make conscience, he will labor to bring them to make conscience where they need not make conscience. He does not care whether you will be remiss or superstitious, so long as you are one of them. If he cannot get you to follow the Epicureanism of the world, as Libertines in diet and apparel, he will make you so precise as to think it a heinous sin to eat one bit of meat or wear one rag of cloth more than is necessary.

How necessary, therefore, it is to sail with an even course, we may guess by other things which will reveal the corruption of our nature. In the time of a plague, we shall see some will be so bold, without any lawful calling or godly warrant, that they will rush into infected places. Then falling sick, their conscience pricks them for their tempting of God by unadvised boldness, in the hour of their death. Others, plunged as deeply in a quite contrary extreme, are too fearful when they do but hear of the sickness, and from sheer fear have been brought to death's door, only by imagining themselves to have been infected when they have been most free. Those often have even died, and that without any natural cause that ever could be known, but only through immoderate fear, and the judgment of God coming upon them for their infidelity and unbelief. It is in this way with us in Christianity, in that as well the oppressing of ourselves with too much fear to be overcome, as the carnal security, in not fearing to be overcome, may bring sin upon us. God's children must labor for a measure, and that must be sought for in the Word, which will teach them how they shall neither decline to the right hand nor to the left but will guide them in the narrow way, showing in everything what is virtue, what is vice; what is the mean, what is the extreme.

Among many examples, let us consider zeal, a most precious virtue in Christianity, so long as it is free from the extremes. Otherwise, if we are cold in zeal, it is a sin on the left hand; if we are zealous without knowledge, it is preposterous and becomes a sin on the right hand.

But can we not come to some perfection? No, if you understand it as an absolute unspottedness; although to that perfection which the Scripture takes for soundness, truth, and sincerity of heart, which is void of careless remissness, we may come. Neither does the Lord deal with us after our sins, nor reward us after our iniquities. In His eyes, the most glorious actions of men are but as waters flowing purely from the Conduit but defiled by passing through a filthy channel. Therefore, having these imperfections, let us not seek to be more righteous than we can be, saying for every error of this life, "Oh, I am none of God's sons, I am none of His daughters; for I cannot find that perfection in me which is to be required." But let us comfort ourselves in the truth of our hearts, and singleness of our desires to serve God, because He is God; and so we shall be accepted by God.

I speak this to this end, that poor souls might have comfort, and know that if they abhor sin as sin, if they examine themselves for it, if they groan under it, if they dislike themselves for it, if they fear to fall into it; the Lord will not pursue them with the rigor of His law, but will give them the sweetness of His promises; they are no more under the curse but under grace.

But further to enforce our exhortation to avoid too scrupulous a fear, which hinders the true examination of our hearts, let us think that it happens in the spiritual conflict as in civil wars. We read that many cities lying in great security have suddenly both been assaulted and overthrown. Also, some countries, too negligent in the means, through excessive fearfulness, have encouraged their enemies with more greedy violence to prey upon them. With which kind of desperate fearfulness, many in the spiritual battle are so seized, that either they stand still and use no means, or else they give over all means and wholly despair. Neither of these are good in the Christian fight. For either in security, we sleep until sin overtakes us, or in desperation, we lay ourselves open for sin to seize us.

Therefore, let us beware of these two extremes, and let us take up the right means of examining our hearts, to know our state by grace, that we may not *abuse* grace. Let us not only examine ourselves for what we have been, or for what we are, but also for what we may be. For if we do not look to ourselves and our ways, we may be where we least think, and become what we least expect. Therefore, let us make sure that we do not abuse grace, so that we may never lose grace. For many in the

Church are like the birds that when they have the light all around them, they sleep in it; but when the night comes, they fly abroad. Thus, many in the time of light and the clear shining of the word upon them, they fall asleep in security. But when the night of desertion comes, then they bestir themselves with sinful ways.

To help against these dangerous extremes, let us be careful to attend to those things which God has *appointed* for us. Let us seek those things that pertain to our peace, which are all summed up in Christ, in whom we have all fullness of blessings. Let us keep our hearts with all diligence, for out of it are the issues of life, and let us pray for that Spirit, which can quicken our dead hearts, to guide our feet into the way of peace.

Common practice teaches us further that when we can hear the Word without trembling at God's judgments, when we can pray without any fear before the Majesty of God, when we can approach the discipline of the Church without any reverence for the Lord's ordinance; all is in vain. Moreover, if we listen with too much trembling, we will learn nothing; if we pray with too servile a fear, our worship of God will be without any comfort and uncheerful. Thus, if we neither minimize sin that is genuinely sin, nor make sin out of what is not truly sin, it is good to proceed to this threefold examination, and to lay the edge of this doctrine closer to our affections, because many will be sound in their maturity of knowledge and barrenness of conscience, able to speak, argue, and proclaim all these things skillfully, which flickering in the periphery of the brain and not residing at the core of the heart, do seal a more just sentence of condemnation against them. To remedy this evil, we must *meditate* deeply on the Law and the Gospel, along with everything related to both, so that finding ourselves far from God's blessings promised to those who keep the law, and seeing ourselves near to the curses due to those who break the law, we may stir up some sense of sin within ourselves. However, we must not stop here but must take a further step: for some, through careful examination of the law, have come to recognize sin within themselves and have seen their own condemnation clearly; yet because they did not strive to see their guilt acquitted through Christ's forgiveness of sin, they cast themselves into a bottomless sea of sorrows. Others, having advanced this far, still come up short and miss the mark; for besides sensing sin pardoned by Christ's death, they did not feel the virtue of His suffering killing sin within them, but saw that with the remission of sin was not joined the mortification of sin; they feared there was no forgiveness for them, and continued to languish in sorrow, feeling themselves still charged with their former guilt. Indeed, some have never truly been taught or firmly grounded in Christ's death and resurrection, not recognizing the power flowing from His death to destroy sin in them, nor the virtue to pardon sin in them; not feeling strength for sanctification coming from Christ's resurrection, as they were convinced of justification and righteousness therein. They have remained, still bleeding at heart, in such a way that their wound of grief could hardly or never be stopped. Therefore, let us fortify our weak souls with this six-fold cord of consolation against these bitter attacks. Let us first work to know sin, then to sorrow for sin, afterward to feel our sins in Christ forgiven, further to look for power to crucify them, then to grasp justification by His resurrection, and finally, hope for strength to proceed from there, to further us in sanctification and holiness of life, even to the end. And that's all briefly for the second thing which we matched with the examination of sin, even the trial of faith: both of which, rightly used, will to some degree protect us from the trouble of an afflicted mind.

    Now let us move quickly to the third part of our division, to show how God's children, having fallen into this spiritual wound, may be *lifted* out of it, which (God willing) we will also accomplish, after we have answered a necessary objection that might seem to oppose us. No one will deny that David, Job, and other saints of God, had a vision of their sins, a sorrow for their sins, and a taste of the remission of their sins: so how did it happen that these men were so troubled in mind? To this I answer, that their trouble came upon them either for failing in some of these aforementioned things, or else they were rather afflicted to test their faith, rather than to punish sin in them. And therefore, let it always be considered that we don't think every struggle of conscience is continually and primarily for the pursuit of our sins; but sometimes and mainly, that it comes for the testing of our faith, and yet secondarily or less principally for the chastising of sin, as we can see in Job. Therefore, let all be warned, when they see good men in this way humbled and brought low in mind, to refrain from saying, "Surely these men are but hypocrites, doubtless these men are great sinners, the Lord has discovered their hypocrisy." For good reason, such silence should be maintained: for the Lord may as well be testing their faith as taking punishment for their sins. If such affliction were always and chiefly sent for sin, then it would follow that all others, as they exceeded them in sin, would also surpass them in the punishment of sin.

But now coming to the healing of this wound, my method of treatment may seem very strange and will be all the more remarkable since my way of proceeding differs from most people in this matter. I'm well aware that many who visit those with troubled consciences continually cry out, "Oh comfort them, oh speak joyful things to them." Indeed, there are some, even among the most learned, who in such cases are filled with these and similar words. "Why are you so downcast, my brother? Why are you so sad, my sister? Be of good cheer; don't take it so hard. What is there that you should fear? God is merciful; Christ is a Savior." These are indeed loving words, but they often do as much good for the troubled soul *as if one were to pour cold water into their chests.* Without further examination of their wounds, they might as easily cause harm as help. Just as nourishing and invigorating medicines are not good for every sick person, especially when the body needs more of a thorough cleansing rather than something restorative, and just as medicines that promote healing may temporarily relieve pain but later make the suffering more intense, so too the comforting application of God's promises are not profitable for everyone who is humbled. Especially when their souls need to be cast down further rather than raised up, those sacred consolations may temporarily heal the conscience and alleviate present grief, but may later make the pain more acute, and the grief may grow greater. The effect of this is that comfort seems to cure for a while, but due to a lack of wisdom in correctly identifying the cause, people apply the wrong remedy, and so from lack of skill, the subsequent fit may be more painful than the former. Some people, without any guidance or practice, become their own physicians. As soon as the fit comes upon them, they think it best to chase away their sorrow by drinking at taverns, engaging in merry company, purging melancholy with medicine—all of which may seem to alleviate the pain for a while, but afterward, it bites more deeply. When their spirits shake them with a second recurrence, since they were not truly examined, purged, and lanced before, the second relapse becomes more dangerous than the first impression.

To return to our purpose, we must understand that all griefs are either confused or distinct, and the mind is either alarmed for a known and certain cause or something unknown and uncertain. For those troubled with such vague griefs, for which they see no reason—as often happens to God's children in secret providence, who either never knew God or only had a general knowledge of Him—I would say that while I don't deny that medicine may be administered if it partially comes from a natural cause, I also urge the use of the word to reveal the principal and original cause in the soul. I emphasize this to ensure wisdom is applied both to the body, if needed, and chiefly to the soul, which so few consider. If a person troubled in conscience goes to a minister, he may focus entirely on the soul and neglect the body. If he goes to a physician, he may only consider the body and neglect the soul. For my part, I would never want the physician's counsel ignored nor the minister's efforts overlooked; since the soul and body dwell together, it is fitting that as the soul is cured by the word, prayer, fasting, threatening, or comforting, the body should also be brought to some balance by medicine, purging, diet, restoration, music, and other means. However, it should always be done in the fear of God and the wisdom of His spirit, not to smother or obscure our troubles with ordinary means, but to use them as preparatives so both our souls and bodies may be more receptive to the spiritual means that follow.

As we require these things for our ministry in such confusion, we wish those who administer to be learned men of sound judgment, wise, experienced in godliness, gentle, and possessing loving spirits. When the troubled patient is persuaded of our knowledge and discretion and senses our tender and loving affection, I believe an entrance is made, and all prejudice is removed. This allows us to work more freely on the conscience, first bringing them to the sight of sin as some cause of their trouble. In this, we must strive to dispel all confusion and blindness of sorrow, endeavoring with wisdom to lead the wounded to some specific object or cause of their trouble. In doing so, we draw out the confession of several, special, and secret sins. I say several and secret sins because I know how many, either through palpable blindness or disordered discernment of sin, talk of nothing so much as of sin; yet they either cannot *describe* specific sins or will not *admit* their secret sins. The former comes from ignorance of the law of God, and the latter from self-love, which makes us loath, even in our mental anguish, to shame ourselves.

Now that the confession of particular sins is required, it can be seen in the 32nd Psalm, in which (being a Psalm of instruction concerning the forgiveness of sins) the Prophet teaches us through his own experience that he could find no relief from his sickness until he had remembered and confessed his sins.

What? Shall we think that the Prophet of God in the psalms (who was taught so wonderfully by the word and by the Spirit) did not see his sins before he preached? Let it be far from us. Rather, let us understand that he had not individually and specifically opened up his sins before the Lord in a distinct confession of them. Although the Lord knows them far better than we ourselves do, such kind of sacrifice is most acceptable to Him.

Now, if in this trouble the people humbled cannot come to a specific insight into sin within themselves, it is good to use the help of others, to whom they may present their hearts to be measured and examined, and their lives to be more deeply scrutinized, by hearing the various articles of the Law explained to them. By this, they may test the entire course of their actions. For (as we mentioned earlier) the grossest hypocrites will generally complain about sin, and yet, when you deal with them regarding specific points of the particular precepts, and test them in the application of things to be done or not done to their own consciences, we shall see many of these poor souls tossed to and fro, now floating in joys, now sunk in sorrows, unable to distinguish one sin from another.

Now, when we see the wound of the spirit arise from any certain and known sin, it is either for some sin already committed, in which we are involved, or else for some sin not yet committed but to which we are tempted. As for the former, it often pleases God to bring old sins to mind when we had not thoroughly repented of them earlier, so that, by representing them to us anew, we might grow to dislike them more. But this is not all. It's not enough just to dislike ourselves for certain details, although it is good to focus on some specific sins;

for just as it is not sufficient to avoid hypocrisy by seeing sin generally, so it is not enough to avoid being deceived by the heart by constantly focusing on one specific sin, and to forget our great and general sins. Instead, let us learn from the specifics to move to the generalities. When a particular sin pursues you, don't only rest in that, but rather say to yourself; "Oh Lord, is this one sin so grievous? And does my God punish this one sin so harshly? How great then should be my punishment, if You should (O Lord) deal with me so for all my other sins." Let us strive to have a sense of both general and specific sins, lest over time our grief passes without benefit, while not being displeased equally with one sin as with another. We either look too superficially at the general sins, without considering the specific ones, or we observe the specifics too superstitiously, ignoring the general sins.

    Regarding the sins to which we are tempted, such as when a man is moved to think blasphemously about God the Father, or to doubt whether there is a Christ, or to imagine coarsely about the Holy Spirit, or to deny God, or to doubt the Trinity, or to be tempted to murder, adultery, or similar things, in which temptations he feels God's spirit rebuke him for them, so he does not know what to do in this situation. On the one hand, he does not dare willingly listen to these terrifying and monstrous temptations; and on the other hand, he fears that in time, through prolonged enticement, he might succumb to them, or at the very least, he does not see how to be freed from them. I think these urges are not to be debated so much as they should provoke us to a more fervent and extraordinary *zeal* in *prayer.*

These are indeed dangerous temptations and should not be kept secret, a tendency to which our nature easily inclines. Instead, they are to be specifically confessed by us. The devil will sometimes come to you to keep you stuck in a general acknowledgment of sin, urging you in this manner: "Surely you must commit this sin, you see you can't have any peace until you have consented, you are destined for it; the reason why you are so incessantly tempted is that you do not yet indulge your desire. Go ahead, deny God, do not believe His word; it's just a strategy to keep people in awe; Religion is not as significant as people consider it." In this way, for fear of yielding on one hand, and for shame of revealing the temptations on the other, many men have wasted away, nearly overcome by them. If we were to reveal this (these men say), what would people think of us? They would label us as atheists and consider us the most wicked people in the world. However, for our instruction and comfort in this matter, let us learn that these kinds of temptations are either corrections for past sins or punishments for present sin, or warnings of a sin to come. We shall see many tempted to adultery, who (undoubtedly) cannot be led to commit it; yet because in their youth they have done so and not repented, it returns to them. The same may be observed in theft, gluttony, and other temptations, which are not so much sent to us to overcome us immediately, but rather to remind us that at some point in the past, having been defeated by them, we should now repent for them. Sometimes a person will be caught in a sin, of which when he will not be warned, neither by public nor private means, then some other strange temptation different from his current sin will befall him, to warn him of that other sin. Like when a worldly person is tempted to adultery, something he has no desire to do; yet it is to make him attend to his worldliness, of which he has such a strong and profound liking; with which, if he will not be awakened, he may suddenly fall into that too, and thus by God's punishment, in punishing one sin with another, both his sins shall be exposed to his great shame, and one sin shall reveal another. Sometimes it also happens that one shall be tempted with such a sin, neither in the past nor presently has he given any favor or reception to; yet the Lord by it may warn him how he might fall into it in the future, and also to demonstrate that he has stood all his former life, more by the grace of God than by the strength of flesh and blood. Therefore, when you are moved to doubt God, Christ, the Word, or justification, do not stand marveling at these strange temptations as much as you think to yourself that it is God's mercy to lead you by them to better discern those temptations in others. When you have observed with fear and trembling how they first enter a person's heart, how they gather strength, how they align with our corrupt nature, in what degrees they grow, how the spirit of God resists them, what the best means are to prevail against them. And thus, if you learn from them, you shall so wonderfully examine and discern through various channels the body, age, and characteristics of these temptations in others, by a holy experience that God has taught you in yourself. Besides laying forth people's hidden corruptions as if you were inside their hearts, you shall also be able to bring an indescribable joy to others who may be tempted as you are now, by showing them that these temptations are not their sins, but their punishments; and that they are rather to be prayed against than debated, and to be more feared than marveled at. You will instruct them that God by such means corrects, warns, and teaches; and that the devil and his minions are constrained to serve God's purposes, even when they intend nothing but our destruction. You will help them to find the depths and causes of these temptations, whether they are corrections for past sins, punishments for the present, or warnings of those that may come. All this knowledge will fill them with unutterable joy, and lead them out of their greatest fears and doubts, showing them how to guard themselves in the future, and how to succor others that are tempted. The matter will be as clear to you as if you were reading from a book, and it shall be useful to them as if it was dictated to them by an angel from heaven.

But some will argue against these things that we have presented. Do you think it a remedy to tear down those who are already humbled? This is more akin to being a butcher than a builder of a person's conscience. To whom I reply that I wish for preachers to be builders and not butchers; and there is a difference between applying something generally and specifically applying the medicine to the wound. It is wise to start by probing first, and to cleanse the wound with the vinegar of the Law, and afterward to soften it with the oil of the Gospel. Both of these must be done *wisely*, using them to some in greater measure and to others in lesser. For just as some, having nothing but a decay of nature and no deadly humor, need restorative rather than purging medicines; others, troubled more by spiritual deficiencies than gross sins, do not need as much the harsh threats of the Law as the sweet promises of the Gospel. Just as the body, having overindulged and suffered a great surfeit not so much weakening nature but threatening imminent death, needs a strong purge rather than comforting and cordial medicines; likewise, the soul, nearly at death's door due to an extraordinary sin, needs to be bored and pierced with the announcement of God's judgments rather than otherwise.

But to speak more plainly and less confusingly, when approaching troubled consciences, we should establish these two principles. First, we must convince the humbled individuals that their sins are forgivable, and their wounds healable. And afterward, that this visitation is not so much a sign of God's wrath and anger as a seal of His mercy and favor, as it is neither blind nor barren but abundant in good effects and fruitful in godly outcomes. How necessary the former is, the experience of almost all who have been brought low is sufficient witness. They have had this attached to their temptations, believing that no one has ever been as afflicted as they, that they alone have faced such temptations, and that God will surely destroy them in some strange and unknown way. In this, they resemble those who have fallen into a dangerous disease and, thinking themselves beyond the reach of the physician's skill and unrecoverable, add a second and more intense grief to their former pain.

Therefore, just as those who seem to be half-healed when someone with experience who has cured a similar malady in others is brought in, these sorrowful souls are refreshed and strengthened with hope, looking for relief when they realize no other temptation has overtaken them than such as have fallen on others and found mercy at the hands of God, inspiring reverence. With this foundation laid, it is good to build up and restore the joy of the mind, partly by the law, to prepare for these joys if the mind, not truly humbled, is unfit to be truly comforted; and partly by the Gospel, if the conscience, kindly brought low, is ready to receive the sweet promises of God in Jesus Christ.

And here again, in response to those who deny that the law should be used at all when we wish to comfort someone, I ask if it is necessary to maintain the righteousness of Christ, is it not also necessary to preserve the righteousness of the law? For seeing that the righteousness of the law, unfulfilled by us, will lead us to the righteousness of Christ imputed to us; and since the righteousness of Christ imputed to us is never fully and truly esteemed until we see the righteousness of the law unperformed by us. Furthermore, if our Savior Christ foretold His disciples that the first work of the Holy Spirit at His coming would be to convict the world of sin, to show that without Jesus Christ there is nothing but sin, and then to rebuke the world of righteousness, that they might see how Christ died not for His sins but for others; I don't see why it would not be very fitting first to reveal the righteousness of the law that people may see their sins; and then the righteousness of Christ, that they may see their sins forgiven in Him. Moreover, where the Lord says through His prophet, "At whatever time a sinner repents of his sins from the bottom of his heart, I will put all his wickedness out of my remembrance," it can be inferred that there must first be genuine sorrow for sin; and then true joy of sins pardoned may be more freely hoped for and expected afterward (Ezekiel 18:21-22). Also, considering all the promises of God in the Gospel are offered to us under the titles and terms of restoring sight to the blind, hearing to the deaf, strength to the lame, health to the sick, and life to the dead; it is evident not only that there is no soul disease that Christ cannot heal but also that we must first find ourselves blind, deaf, mute, lame, sick, and dead before He will deal with us; because those who are whole do not need the Physician, and He came to call sinners, not the righteous to repentance (Matthew 9:12-13).

Now, to do this wisely, neither oppressing the conscience too severely nor easing it too recklessly, it will be a safe way to use the well-measured words of the Apostle to the sorcerer, "Repent, that if it be possible, your sin may be forgiven you," (Acts 8:22). Here he does not wholly discourage him, because it may be his sin may be pardoned; nor does he encourage him too boldly, showing that without repentance, it is entirely impossible to be forgiven.

And so that we are not overly hasty in our comfort, let us be warned by the blasphemous speech of that *detestable* Arian, who in recent years was executed in Norwich. This hellish heretic, just before he was to be executed, shed a few insincere tears, asking whether he could be saved in Christ or not? When one told him that if he truly repented, he would not perish, he broke out monstrously into this speech: "Is your Christ so easily entreated indeed, as you say? Then I defy Him and do not care for Him." Oh, how good it would have been not to have thrown this precious stone to this swine? How safe to have stood by the sobriety of the apostle: "If it be possible, the thoughts of your heart may be forgiven you."

To summarize the practical application of this entire discourse, as we must not keep the balm of Gilead from those that have wounds; neither must we cast it upon those who have nothing but a decay of nature, and no festering or deadly humor, need to be eased by such strong medicines. If we find those who are terrified and perplexed in conscience, partly by the wound of sin and partly by the fear of God's judgment, we may be ready to comfort them with the glad tidings of the Gospel. If we find others, again, puffed up with conceit of their own righteousness and need to be humbled, we may terrify them with the Law's curse. But both of these must be wisely done, knowing how to distribute both Law and Gospel, comfort and terror, according to the several conditions and needs of men's consciences.

In this way, we may hope that this disease, so fearful in name and nature, will by God's blessing be prevented in many, cured in some, and alleviated in all. To Him who has the keys of David, who opens and no man shuts, and shuts and no man opens, who binds and loosens all things both in heaven and earth, be all praise and glory, world without end.

But before we move further into this sea of specific temptations and begin to explore the perilous passages of natural corruption and original sin, the troubling froth of which almost overwhelms many poor pilgrims, it will be good to give this caution. Both in these and in the previous troubles, men would do well to be repeatedly reminded to bear *patiently* with a wounded spirit, even if they become somewhat irritable. This patience is warranted, seeing that the Holy Spirit speaks so favorably of them, saying, "A wounded spirit who can bear?" (Proverbs 18:14). And surely our practice in other matters, according to the law of equity, may demand this of us. For if men, guided by the light of reason, can recognize the duty to not respond furiously but rather to tolerate meekly and wisely the rash speeches of a man whose mind is disturbed by a burning fever or similar violent and vehement sickness, then we may easily infer, using the same rule of reason, not to judge too harshly the impatient words of someone who, by reason of a parching spiritual fever, is unsettled in all parts of his mind and has all the veins of his heart (as it were in a spiritual agony) troubled.

Therefore, both lacking in godly wisdom for want of taste, and lacking in Christian love for want of charity, are the murmuring objections of those who say, "What? Is this the godly man? Is this the one so troubled for his sins? Why, see how irritable he is; nothing can please him, nobody can satisfy him." Consider, O man, if you can bear with a frail body, that you must much more bear with a frail mind. Consider, Oh man, that his irritability wounds him to the heart more than any injury you could afflict him with. And therefore, seeing that he torments his own soul over it, you need not add anything to his affliction and to exacerbate his painful hurt. Consider that it is a blessed thing to mercifully contemplate the state of the needy, and that to aggravate a fresh wound or to strain a bleeding sore is nothing else but to bring new torment, like Job's friends, where there is no need for it.

Just as a wise father rather pities than rebukes his child when, due to sickness, the child's appetite is not easily satisfied, so, if we intend to do any good with an afflicted mind, we must not be stern in reprimanding every weakness, but compassionate in contemplating its delicate frailty. I do not say this to nurture irritability in anyone, but would instead encourage them to strive for patience and to seek peace. Even if they do not find it at first, they must wait on the Lord through prayer and say, "Lord, because there is mercy with thee, that thou mayest be feared, I will wait for thee, as the eyes of servants look unto the hand of their masters," (Psalm 130:4; 123:2). "I will condemn myself for my folly and say, Oh my soul, why art thou so heavy? Why art thou so cast down within me? Still trust in the Lord, for he is thy health and thy salvation."

FINIS.

The Second Treatise for An Afflicted Conscience

In all afflictions, God's children must look to the end; they should desire to gain from them and in them seek the way of true comfort and consolation. To find this, they must understand that the afflictions of the godly are *temporary*, serving them as remedies and medicines, with an *always* happy end. In them, they are not only preserved and purified from many sins, but also greatly adorned with the image of Jesus Christ, who is the eldest Son in the house of God. Moreover, the suffering of true Christians is a sweet and lovely call from God to repentance, reminding us to consider our debts, since we tend to think the day of reckoning is still far away. Indeed, we fall asleep until our time is up, and while God extends our days waiting for our repentance, we never consider our sins until the hour arrives when we die in disgrace.

The best way to greet the Lord's visitation is to immediately and sincerely *pray* for our sins to be forgiven. The Lord often shackles us with His chastisements because we care more about relieving our sickness than being freed from our sin. We are reluctant to admit this, as we don't want to be seen under God's wrath. Some, when hearing of their sins during affliction, will indeed admit their weaknesses, but they have no true remorse to restrain themselves from sin, because their understanding of it is confused. And even if they are tossed and tormented, they do not think that God is in control. These men, if God tolerates them, become complacent in their sins. Prosperity lulls us into a false sense of security, and when God leaves us alone, we convince ourselves that we are in His favor and loved by Him because He doesn't punish us. In this way, we are reckless, measuring God's love by our own feelings.

In this, we reveal our ignorance of suffering's purpose, as affliction brings humility, which leads to repentance, and repentance to mercy. Some, when faced with God's fearful judgment, have fleeting thoughts about their sins and Christ's suffering, but at other times they shut their minds and hearts, feeling no genuine sorrow. They ridicule those who mourn, making light of sin, not considering the agonies that await them either in the hour of death or the day of judgment. They may think they have shown repentance when they sigh once and then pass over God's wrath as if walking on hot coals. Thus, while the Lord generously shows His love in prosperity, they play games with His majesty and make a sport of His mercy.

These imperfections can be corrected if, in our deepest rest, with reverent and humble fear of God's judgments, we await our day of trial and prepare for the Lord's visitations. Recognizing our misery through sin will lead us to feel God's mercy. Once our sin is forgiven, our weaknesses will soon be healed. Therefore, we must first learn to cleanse our souls from sin and then endure our physical ailments. It's certain that if we have allowed our hearts to be stirred by God's judgments and become tender and aware of God's fear, we will recognize our sins, which will bring a sort of sickness to the body and soul, assuring us of our regeneration. Happy are we if we find ourselves so troubled by our sins.

It's true that during our struggles, we may find it hard to differentiate between temptation to evil and consent to it. Evil thoughts can so dominate God's children that, even though they weep, pray, and meditate (which are the last means to relieve them), they may still *feel* them intensely, like a sickness in their bodies. Those thoughts may persist without diminishing, except for any delight in them. Thus, for our comfort in this, we should not torture ourselves with mental unrest because of these wicked thoughts and attacks. Instead, we should calm ourselves and not allow sickness of body or mind to render us unprofitable to ourselves and God's Church. The godly will never be entirely free from sin and will be plagued by evil thoughts, suspicions, delusions, and vain fantasies; the body of sin will remain with us as long as we live. The filthiness of sin bubbles within us, producing a foul stench in our minds, detestable not only to the regenerated mind but also disgusting even to the natural man, who would recoil from such a repulsive pit of sin and iniquity. It often weakens us and, if it could, would corrupt even the regenerated part. Sin is powerful and furious, but we must not cease to mourn for our sins or despair, even if our sorrow is slight. If we are sorrowful for our heart's hardness, if we can grieve that we are not more grieved, if we can sigh and groan under the weight of our iniquities, it is a greater comfort to us and a greater testimony that our faith is sincere which may be lacking, by occasion; in the same way, the Lord God, our most gracious Father, does not reject us because, through our imperfections, we are unable or afraid to draw near to the throne of grace; but rather pities us. Seeing us from a distance and desiring to come to Him, He meets us on our way and, with the grace and strength of His own hand, directs our steps towards His kingdom. Just as one who freely plans to give a wedge of gold will not take back his gift because the hand of the person who should receive it is weak, troubled with gout, palsy, or leprosy, as long as the person is able to hold it, even if in great weakness. Similarly, the Lord, planning in free mercy to bestow on us an immortal weight of glory, will not deprive us of it, though many filthy blemishes have polluted and weakened our faith, so that in any small measure we are able to take hold of His promises. We should not look for the perfection of faith because we never believe as we should; but rather on that which the Gospel offers and gives, and on God's mercy and peace in Christ. If we can lay our heads in Christ's lap, like Saint John, then we are in happiness, security, and perfect quietness. On the other hand, some people, even though a tormented conscience is a stinging serpent, and even though it would be better if all creatures rose up against us with their poison rather than once come before the fearful face of God, are so dull that they are entirely hardened. If they are afflicted with sickness, they cry out in pain; if they are troubled with poverty, they can complain; but as for torment of mind, they cannot understand it, and to speak of a bruised, contrite, and broken heart is strange to them. As evidence, our consciences are lulled to sleep so that not one among a thousand knows what it is to be pressed and torn by God's judgment. But blessed are those who feel this in their bodies for their own salvation, while sin may be both punished and purged. Although God may spare us for a time, we know what He holds for our *end*. Therefore, it's best for us to run to the Lord in this life with a troubled mind, lest we wait until the Lord has confined us with heavy chains of despair when He will summon us to the judgment seat in the sight of His angels. Then, assembling the great jury of His saints against us, He will announce our fearful and final sentence of eternal condemnation. For we see many who have been careless and have feasted all their life long. And when people have tried to make them feel God's judgment, they have turned it all into mockery, but the Lord has so reduced their joy as they approach death that instead of resting and playing (to which they had been given), they have felt the terror of death, hell, and damnation. Wrapping up their joys in final despair, they have forced out curses against their filthy pleasures. Therefore, if we in the tempest of our temptations will sail the right course, neither shrinking nor slipping into the gulf of despair nor crashing our vessel against the rock of presumption, let us cry to the Lord with a contrite spirit:

"Have mercy upon me, heal my soul, for I have sinned against thee, forgive all mine iniquities, and heal all mine infirmities. Thou healest those that are broken in heart, and bindest up their wounds. Why art thou cast down my soul, and why art thou disquieted within me, wait on God, for I will yet give Him thanks, He is my present help, and my God. Yet my soul, keep thou silence before God, from Him comes my salvation, He is my strength, therefore I shall not be much moved. His mightiness is enough to give me courage, even when I am forsaken, I know that the diminishing of my body, goods, friends, or anything else is a call to that which will never diminish or decay. I believe that my Lord and my God entices me daily toward it, so that I might not doubt that when my body is laid in the grave, and there consumed as if to nothing, yet my soul, resting in the Lord's bosom, will return to me and rise to glory, just as it did rise to grace by resting in this life in Christ's mercies. Truly I see, and that with joy, that my flesh must decay; whatever freshness was in it diminishes day by day. I need not go far to seek death, for I feel not so small an infirmity in my body but the same is a messenger of dissolution. Yet despite all this, I shall see my God, and when I am covered in the belly of the grave with earth, I am assured that He will reach me His hand to lift me again to the beauty of His inheritance; so that this small cottage and shed of leaves, being brought to the grave, shall be carried into an incorruptible tabernacle."

Thus, by communicating with our hearts and being still in the peace of a good conscience concerning our outward sufferings, we will find that the Lord, through His fatherly and loving chastisements, intends nothing more than to test our obedience (as good reason it is that He should) and to confirm our faith, which is also most necessary. However, as I said, He uses a fatherly correction, that is, in mercy, measure, and judgment. For although His corrections are painful wounds to flesh and blood, they are *sovereign* medicines to the soul and conscience, especially when the Lord gives us the privilege of His children, that by His Holy Spirit He overcomes us, lest we finally become His judge and He not ours. And for this reason, the Lord is often provoked to put on as it were an opposite face and lock us up in a prison of adversity to restrain us from the liberty of our sins, which Satan would have us violently rush into. Truly, though the wisdom of the flesh persuades us that nothing is better than to be spared, and not to be spied upon when the Lord calls us to account, yet the Spirit, showing our desperate state without the sieve of affliction and the filter of adversity, teaches us that of all God's blessings, we cannot sufficiently esteem this one, being the mother of humility and the nurse of true repentance. Again, the Lord often, by inward temptations and outward crosses, draws us from the stake of security and reluctance to good works; lest in time we lose the experience of our knowledge and faith in Christ, and seek some easier kind of life for flesh and blood. We cannot truly repent until, by some cross, we know this world to be a place of sorrow and not of mirth and delight. For as long as we make our prosperity a barrier to beat down all harms, we must expect adversity to beat down the high sail of our proud hearts, by which we chase after our lusts and leave behind the anchor of peace, which is our trust in God. Let us learn then, when the world begins to favor us, and we have, as it were, a hundred thousand soldiers to fight for us, let us then learn to distrust our strengths, lest our soul say to us, "Look what an army of hope, what forces and helps, what comforts and pleasures, what riches and pleasures you have gathered for yourself." When we look in this way, we will leave behind God's protecting grace and put ourselves under the tutorship of the flesh. If we lose our faith, our daily study, our inward humility, our meditations of mortality, our constant repentance, our fear of God's judgments, and our quick and zealous obedience to God's commandments, we will fall into a carnal security where all the angels of heaven cannot retrieve us until, by some heavy cross or affliction, the Lord stops us on our way to hell. Now, to be safe, I mean not to be free from all the darts of Satan or the chains of the flesh, nor to be delivered from the troubles of the world, nor to be spared the rod of the cross; but rather to have Christ Jesus as our Captain, and to wait on His hand to lead us out of the battle, to direct our ways in the wilderness, to keep us safe from sin, Satan, the world, the flesh, and all our enemies, until He brings us into the heavenly Jerusalem, there to reign with Him forever in glory everlasting.

It is fitting for the Lord to change our situation so that we don't become entrapped in the gifts of prosperity and become so foolish as not to continue on our path to eternal life. Our natural inclination is to *forget* that we are on earth as travelers; to jump up into the clouds, and to promise ourselves that our entire lives will be prosperous. As long as God leaves us at ease, we regard ourselves as if we were minor gods. But when we find ourselves confined, and we don't know the end of our misery, recognizing that we are in this life merely as temporary workers, paid for the present day but uncertain about what will happen the next day, we wish to rest in the bosom of God's providence. Thus, we lower our expectations when the Lord declares war on our secure prosperity, which persuades us that we will live forever and prevents us from reflecting on our frailties and miseries. Therefore, let us fashion our prosperity according to the model of humility and, in our best state, prepare ourselves to suffer adversity. When things are going well, we must expect them to get worse and remain vigilant when God treats us most gently, so that in abundance we may anticipate our needs, in health foresee our sickness, and in prosperity anticipate our calamity. Concerning worldly things, the faithful must be in doubt, fearing that what they hold with one hand may be taken away with the other. We must not think that we will always enjoy our freedom and never experience suffering; instead, we must be prepared to receive punishment from the Lord, knowing that our slightest cries will halt His greatest scourges. Let us expect to be attacked, but not overwhelmingly, because God will help us. Let us expect to fall but only to our knees, because God's hand supports us. Let us expect to be humbled, but mercifully, because the Lord sustains us. Since we are assured that mercy surrounds us on all sides, it's our duty to continuously confess before the Lord that we constantly give Him new reasons to punish us, and that our sins often push away the wings of God's mercy, under which we have long been comforted. God's children recognize unceasingly that God has rods ready, even though they see no immediate evil, to beat them away from their sins. They focus all their care on how they may suffer adversity for God's glory, rather than sleep securely in prosperity for their own pleasure.

    When the Lord puts us on the *torturous rack* for the reasons mentioned, we must pray to Him that even though He keeps us under pressure, we may have moments to reflect on our days of pleasure and to examine our ingratitude, which closes the door of God's mercy to us. And since our afflictions are more painful when they touch the soul, we must resolve to continue on our journey, despite seeing nothing but thorns of temptation and briars of evil affection. Though we must sometimes leap over barriers, rocks, and ditches, we must not stop serving God. For if we were always in a fair meadow, running by the water's side in the shade, with nothing but pleasure and joy all our life, who could boast that they had served God with genuine affection? But when God sends us things contrary to our desires, so that we must sometimes enter into a mire and at other times march upon ragged rocks and stones, then we will make use of a well-practiced mind in prayer, repentance, and contempt for this life. Why does the Lord sometimes let us wither away and languish in continual grief when He could rid us of it at once? Doubtless, it's to make us confess His mercy more freely and acknowledge His justice more acutely. We must now learn to control all the passions of *impatience* by comparing our suffering with God's wondrous mercies and our minor afflictions with the unbearable struggles of our ancestors. There is no greater cause for despair under the cross than when Satan convinces us that no one has ever been treated so harshly or persuades us that although God afflicted the faithful before us, they were not as weak as we are. But let us remember how God treated His servants, those He loved, whose well-being was dear and precious to Him, and how He often brought them to such extremes that they couldn't look up or speak or remain silent. In case our weaknesses overpower us and temptations confuse us, let us remember the Saints of God, who were compelled to bow under God's hand with sighs and groans; whose martyrs and tormented children should be our mirrors, teaching us that as God gives the gifts of the Spirit, He sends greater afflictions to make them more esteemed and to cause a more abundant fruit of their faith. How did God deal with Abraham, not an ordinary man but more like an angel, whose tenth part of suffering would make a stout heart falter? How was David, God's servant, trained in God's school, who felt all of God's arrows shot at him? It's necessary for God's graces not to lie idle in His children but be set to work by afflictions, so that they may be recognized at the right time and place. How did God act like a lion with Hezekiah, who, as with paws and teeth, bruised and crushed his bones; not so that we may accuse God of cruelty but that we may see with what anguish the Lord sometimes exercises His holy servants, and with what patience He arms them. Even in their severe trials, they rely on God, accusing themselves, saying, "I will bear the wrath of the Lord because I have sinned against Him," and excusing the Lord with all humility with David, Psalm 119:75, "I know, O Lord, that thy judgments are right, and that thou in faithfulness hast afflicted me."

It's also beneficial to our spiritual growth and Christian patience to occupy our hearts with thoughts of mourning even in our greatest feasting and to turn our minds to *serious reflections* on adversity when present pleasures would most divorce us from remembering it. In this way, though we have much in possession, we'll have little in affection, and when God elevates us the most, we will fear our lack of humility. Especially when the Lord enriches us most with His blessings, we should be questioning and judging ourselves for how we use God's creatures. Often, He gives in judgment what He might deny in mercy, and often denies in love what He might give in anger.

FINIS

The Marks of a Righteous Man

A righteous person possesses three distinct privileges. First, they will never perish, even though afflictions frequently befall them. In fact, when there are many of these righteous individuals, the Lord will spare their dwelling places for their sake. Secondly, when the Lord intends to bring destruction upon a land or country, He will first either take the righteous through death or relocate them elsewhere. This is reminiscent of what happened to Lot, and the children of Israel when Pharaoh was overthrown. Thirdly, the Lord's response to the wicked is not so much punishment as it is favor for the sake of the godly. Even if the righteous experience the same temporal trials, these circumstances draw them closer to heaven, while the ungodly are cast down to hell. This is akin to using a flail to separate chaff for burning and preserving pure grain.

Some individuals believe that there are no righteous people. This belief arises either from ignorance or from observing the sins and loose conduct of others. However, this contradicts the Scriptures, which indeed describe some as righteous. Such a belief would render Christ's sacrifice meaningless, implying that there is no salvation, as salvation is offered only to the righteous.

Others think that righteousness is an inherent quality and that we can achieve perfect righteousness through works. This was believed by the Pelagians, contemporary Papists, and those of the Family of Love.

Yet, the testimonies of Scriptures that describe all our righteousness as *stained* garments (Isa. 64:6), our inability to answer even one out of a thousand charges, and the sins of those regarded as righteous in the Word, argue otherwise. Abraham sinned after being declared righteous: he doubted God's providence, had relations with his maidservant, lied, and led his wife into sin. Similarly, Lot strayed from Abraham, with whom the covenant was made, without just cause; he was reluctant to leave Sodom and engaged in sinful acts with his daughters. David, Job, Zechariah, Noah, Peter, and the tax collector also sinned, despite being justified by faith just like Abraham, who believed in God.

As a middle ground, some emphasize righteousness through faith without works but lead unrighteous lives. They have formulated a kind of righteousness that is common among dissolute Protestants. This concept will become clearer when we define what constitutes *a righteous person*.

True righteousness is *imputed* righteousness. To attain this, we must first recognize and acknowledge our lack of righteousness and our fullness of unrighteousness due to our sins. This was the reason Paul considered his previous righteousness as worthless. Secondly, feeling the weight of our sins, we must desire to forsake them and be liberated from the punishment they deserve. Thirdly, by faith, we must turn to Christ, seeking to have His righteousness credited to us, our sins forgiven, and not imputed to us. This is illustrated by the example of the Publican, and also of Abraham. Christ acts as a Mediator when we are wounded by the sword of the Word. Even though we are justified in Christ, sin still lingers within us (Rom. 7). It should not dominate our mortal bodies, and we must follow Abraham's example, walking in uprightness of heart before the Lord, as Abraham was required to do (Gen. 17:1ff). In this kind of context, David stated that those with no deceit in their spirit were upright, "Be glad in the LORD, and rejoice, ye righteous: and shout for joy, all ye that are upright in heart," (Psa. 32:11). This implies that if one does not walk uprightly, sins still remain.

Uprightness of heart can be measured through four distinct criteria. Firstly, we must love all good things and hate all sins, both in ourselves and others, even if we cannot perfectly fulfill all commandments (Psalm 119:6). Secondly, we should strive to please and glorify God in all our actions, seeking His approval without expecting rewards, even in the face of troubles that result from it. This should be solely to please God and glorify His name, while avoiding evil for the same reason.

The absence of this pure intention led Christ to rebuke the Scribes and Pharisees for fasting and praying to be seen by men (Matt. 23:13ff, 23, 25, 27, 29; Luke 11:44). The lack of this principle also condemns the Papists and the Family of Love in all their actions, as they perform them to achieve righteousness. Once works were deemed a means of justification, people built churches, abbeys, etc., and such deeds were praised. Now, when good deeds are required not for merit but for God's glory and as signs and seals of righteousness, only a few are willing to undertake them, highlighting the scarcity of righteous individuals on earth.

Exceptions apply to this rule as well. Rebellion in the flesh and hypocrisy will certainly emerge. Yet, we must focus on our chief aim and predominant influence, as with other aspects such as complexion. If our conscience attests that our primary concern is pleasing God, our heart is upright even if hypocrisy accompanies it. Distinguishing between doing something out of hypocrisy and doing it mixed with hypocrisy is essential. While we may not yet comprehend all good or evil, much less love the former and hate the latter as we should, if we are not troubled by our infirmities and displeased with ourselves when overtaken by a sin, if we fail to hate sin and love goodness when revealed by the Lord, our corruption will be revealed. The extent to which we *tolerate* sin correlates with the *level* of *hypocrisy* within us. If we grow more distressed with each sin, it indicates uprightness and a possibility of recovering from the fall. The hypocrite, however, behaves contrarily.

The second criterion is that we are primarily concerned with pleasing and glorifying God in all we do. We aim to prove ourselves to Him without expecting rewards, even if trouble arises as a consequence. We shun evil for the sake of pleasing God and glorifying His name.

This principle's absence prompted Christ to rebuke the Scribes and Pharisees for fasting and praying to gain recognition from people. Lack of this *intention* also condemns Papists and the Family of Love in their actions, as they perform them to attain righteousness. When works were seen as a path to justification, individuals constructed churches, abbeys, *etc.*, which received high praise. However, now that good deeds are required not for merit but for God's glory and as signs and seals of righteousness, only a few are willing to undertake them, revealing the scarcity of righteous people on earth.

Exceptions apply to this rule as well. Rebellion in the flesh and hypocrisy will certainly emerge. Yet, we must focus on our chief aim and predominant influence, as with other aspects such as complexion. If our conscience attests that our primary concern is pleasing God, our heart is upright even if hypocrisy accompanies it. Distinguishing between doing something out of hypocrisy and doing it mixed with hypocrisy is essential. While we may not yet comprehend all good or evil, much less love the former and hate the latter as we should, if we are not troubled by our infirmities and displeased with ourselves when overtaken by a sin, if we fail to hate sin and love goodness when revealed by the Lord, our corruption will be revealed. The extent to which we tolerate sin correlates with the level of hypocrisy within us. If we grow more distressed with each sin, it indicates uprightness and a possibility of recovering from the fall. The hypocrite, however, behaves contrarily.

The third indication is that we should never be satisfied with ourselves or our past accomplishments. Instead, we should continuously strive to leave behind sin and draw closer to God. This quality can be observed in the example of Abraham and is recorded in the Book of Proverbs. Furthermore, Paul asserts that those who are mature in their faith share this mindset. In this way, it becomes apparent who either stagnates at the beginning of their spiritual journey or regresses after making some progress. If we have once experienced the goodness of God's grace and then turn away from it, it becomes exceedingly difficult to be renewed through repentance. This is due to two reasons: firstly, such individuals are always learning but never improving, as denounced by the prophet Isaiah who admonished, "precept upon precept, line upon line," (Isa. 28:10).

Secondly, even if they acquire knowledge, they fail to build upon it to maintain a righteous conscience. This lesson is evident in the experience of those who become *heretics*. This notion *terrifies* the godly, who would rather endure all the miseries of Job than succumb to apostasy. Thus, the imperative is to consistently advance, acknowledging what we have accomplished, yet not for self-aggrandizement, but rather acknowledging our deficiencies and offering gratitude for what the Lord has wrought within us. Nevertheless, there are times when children of God perceive their progress as sluggish or even experience grave transgressions. In the former case, if we do not resist, if we are not displeased with ourselves, and if we do not grieve over this state of affairs, we risk the Lord shutting us out. As demonstrated by His punishment for those who do not advance, one can only wonder what fate awaits those who regress. Conversely, if we genuinely lament our sins, struggle against them, and earnestly seek to overcome them, we find solace and hope. Regarding the latter scenario, the Lord utilizes these falls to propel His children forward, to deepen their spiritual journey. Through this process, they become more acutely aware of their inherent corruption, leading to humility. Although it is a dreadful thing for Christians to fall into serious sin, these experiences drive them to turn to Christ with greater urgency. In turn, their falls make them more cautious, spurring them to hasten their pace in the journey, much like runners in a race or travelers in a journey who, after a stumble or delay, redouble their efforts to achieve their goals. For instance, after his fall, David, when confronted with his original corruption, fervently sought the renewal of his spirit (Psalm 51). Thus, although the righteous may fall, the Lord reveals their transgressions to them, and they rise again. Conversely, hypocrites and the wicked persist in their ways and deteriorate further, for salvation is reserved for those who truly love it.

The fourth indication is that we should love righteous individuals and virtuous deeds, both in others and in ourselves. By righteous individuals, I mean those who are our superiors, our peers, or our inferiors. Loving those who are ahead of us encourages emulation, as we strive to become like them. We should not be content with our own qualities and accomplishments but seek to progress further. This idea is supported by the example of Abraham (Gen. 18:19) and underscored in the book of Proverbs. Paul also states that those who are mature in their faith share this mindset. Therefore, it becomes evident who remains at the beginning of their spiritual journey or regresses after making some progress. Should we taste of God's gracious favor and then forsake it, it becomes nearly impossible to be renewed through repentance. Two reasons contribute to this difficulty: firstly, these individuals are always learning but *show* no improvement, as Isaiah, again, rebukes by saying, "precept upon precept, line upon line." Secondly, even if they gain knowledge, they fail to build upon it to maintain a righteous conscience. This lesson is evident in the experience of those who become heretics. This notion terrifies the godly, who would rather endure all the miseries of Job than succumb to apostasy. Hence, the imperative is to consistently advance, acknowledging what we have accomplished, yet not for self-aggrandizement, but rather acknowledging our deficiencies and offering gratitude for what the Lord has wrought within us. Nevertheless, there are times when children of God perceive their progress as sluggish or even experience grave transgressions. In the former case, if we do not resist, if we are not displeased with ourselves, and if we do not grieve over this state of affairs, we risk the Lord shutting us out. As demonstrated by His punishment for those who do not advance, one can only wonder what fate awaits those who regress. Conversely, if we genuinely lament our sins, struggle against them, and earnestly seek to overcome them, we find solace and hope. Regarding the latter scenario, the Lord utilizes these falls to propel His children forward, to *deepen* their spiritual journey. Through this process, they become more acutely aware of their inherent corruption, leading to humility. Although it is a dreadful thing for Christians to fall into serious sin, these experiences drive them to turn to Christ with *greater* urgency. In turn, their falls make them more cautious, spurring them to hasten their pace in the journey, much like runners in a race or travelers in a journey who, after a stumble or delay, redouble their efforts to achieve their goals. For instance, after his fall, David, when confronted with his original corruption, fervently sought the renewal of his spirit. Thus, although the righteous may fall, the Lord reveals their transgressions to them, and they rise again. Conversely, hypocrites and the wicked persist in their ways and deteriorate further, for salvation is reserved for those who truly love it.

FINIS

Sure Signs of Election for Those Who Have Been Brought Low

1. A Clear Understanding of Judgment: Grasping the truth and genuine meaning of the Scriptures, whether they are in our favor or against us.
2. Confronting Sin Internally: Reproving sin within oneself, leading to a spirit of humility and poverty, resulting in mourning. (Matthew 5:3-4)
3. Meekness of Spirit: Humbly prostrating ourselves at the feet of Christ. (Matthew 5:4)
4. Hungering for Christ's Righteousness: A strong desire and high regard for the righteousness found in Christ, surpassing the value of all earthly things. (Philippians 3:8-9)
5. Contemplating and Desiring Heavenly Things: Engaging in thoughtful reflection and expressing a longing to discuss matters of the heavenly realm.
6. Struggle Between Flesh and Spirit: Experiencing the internal conflict between the desires of the flesh and the influence of the spirit, with the practice of allowing the spirit to gain mastery. (Romans 7:23)
7. Nurturing the Spirit: Engaging in sowing to the spirit through the use of spiritual means, such as the Word and prayer.

8. Genuine and Sincere Purpose: Making an unfeigned commitment, empowered by received strength, to consecrate oneself fully for God's glory and the benefit of others.
9. Surrendering to God: Offering oneself wholeheartedly into God's hands.
10. Anticipating Spiritual Growth and Resurrection: Eagerly expecting the continual improvement of one's spiritual well-being and the future resurrection of the body.
11. Forgiving Enemies: Demonstrating the ability to forgive those who have wronged us.
12. Acknowledging Offenses with a Purpose to Leave Them: Admitting and confessing our wrongdoings, with a genuine intention to forsake them.
13. Delighting in God's Saints: Finding joy and delight in the company of fellow believers who are devoted to God.
14. Longing for the Prosperity of God's Church: Expressing a desire for the flourishing and peaceful state of God's Church even after one's own passing.
15. An Upright Spirit: Possessing an honest and sincere heart that consistently seeks to do good, despite the limitations of our weaknesses.

These are indeed certain indicators of our election. Even if someone may fall short in some aspects, let them examine their heart. If there exists a genuine desire and longing for these graces, they can take comfort in remembering passages such as Nehemiah 11, Psalm 10, Psalm 119:6, Psalm 119:40, and Psalm 119:37.

A Treatise on Self-Examination Before and After the Lord's Supper

1 Corinthians 11:28: "So let a man examine himself, and so let him eat of that bread and drink of that cup."

These words are commonplace and widely known. They constitute a decree or ordinance through which the Apostle sets forth the requirement for every person to examine themselves before partaking in the mystery of the Supper. Two main aspects are emphasized in these words: the necessity of examination and the manner in which it should be conducted. Regarding the first aspect, though the phrase "Let a man examine himself" might appear as advice or counsel in our modern language, in the original context, the wording is akin to the language used in enacting laws and decrees in the courts of princes and parliaments. This linguistic nuance makes it clear that what might seem as mere advice is, in fact, a strong injunction. While the command should hold sufficient weight for us to readily comply, once received through faith, we should delve into the reasons behind this stringent examination and discern why it is imperative to execute it.

These reasons can be categorized into two primary points: the requirement emanates either from reflective reverence for the presence of the person we are encountering, akin to how individuals diligently prepare themselves before approaching a dignitary, or it emerges from the extraordinary significance of the benefits received. This later aspect compels us to prepare ourselves, just as we prepare ourselves before consuming medicine to enhance its efficacy. Both these facets come together in the context of the Lord's Supper. Even if we were to disregard the potential benefits, the sheer reverence for the person with whom we partake should suffice to prompt our careful consideration, as we observe individuals earnestly preparing themselves when in the company of esteemed figures. It is analogous to the instruction in Proverbs 23:1, "When thou sittest to eat with a ruler, consider diligently what is before thee." Joseph, for instance, changed his attire and groomed himself before standing before Pharaoh, an action he took not knowing the ultimate purpose or outcome of his appearance. Similarly, in a parable, we learn that not only those who decline but even those who attend the King's banquet without proper attire are rejected, stressing the importance of adequate preparation. This principle equally applies to the Lord's Supper, as it represents the table where our hearts commune within the heavenly realm, with the presence of angelic hosts and the glorious Trinity. Therefore, we are to meticulously prepare ourselves in light of the presence of God the Father, Son, Holy Spirit, and the celestial assembly.

Yet, our preparation must surpass these considerations, considering the elaborate preparation mandated even for lesser matters in the law. Though not explicitly commanded there, the proportional reasoning demands a deep reverence for this occasion. For instance, in the observance of the Passover feast (2 Chro. 35:6), even though its significance pales in comparison to the Gospel's sacred meal, there were several days of preparation. In this way, the inherent respect for participating in the Lord's Supper should lead us to prepare ourselves thoughtfully and with due reverence. Moreover, in comparison to situations where preparation was required, such as the consumption of the showbread or the eating of the Passover lamb, we should, by all means, prepare ourselves in approaching the Lord's table.

It is noteworthy that even if we solely focus on reverence for the person involved, without considering the spiritual benefits, we should, nonetheless, approach the Lord's Supper with utmost preparation. Drawing parallels from examples in the Old Testament, like the reverence exhibited during the eating of the Passover lamb or the respect shown for holy objects, we can deduce the importance of our approach to this sacred event. Even the narrative of Uzzah's demise (2 Sam. 6:3-8) when he touched the Ark without being prepared for the encounter should alert us to the gravity of approaching God's presence *unprepared*. Moreover, if we look back to the instance of Moses removing his shoes in the presence of God or the consecration required for handling snuffers, pans, and candlesticks, we find further evidence that points to the significance of preparation. Following this line of reasoning, our preparation for partaking in the Lord's Supper is unequivocally required.

Furthermore, if we contemplate the meticulous preparations made by Joseph of Arimathea (Mark 15:45) and other devout individuals while attending to Christ's body after His crucifixion, we should feel an even stronger sense of responsibility in approaching the living, glorified body of the Lord during the sacrament. Just as they did not merely cover Christ's body with a clean cloth, but with a clean *syndon*, an exceptionally fine linen, so should our preparation for the Lord's Supper surpass ordinary measures.

But if the Lord were to lower His demand and focus on our own personal practice, disregarding His divine presence's persuasion, we would then consider our own profit. Just as we wouldn't put our common or profane food into an unwashed platter or a cup that hasn't been cleaned, so should we not place the elements representing Christ's body and blood into an unprepared heart and unsanctified soul. Doing so would make the one who puts these sacred elements into an unprepared heart and unsanctified soul most culpable of the judgment pronounced upon those who partake unworthily: "For he that eateth and drinketh unworthily, eateth and drinketh damnation to himself, not discerning the Lord's body," (1 Corinthians 11:29). Our Savior Christ and the Prophets lament that people are skilled in minor matters and human statutes, yet remain ignorant of the core teachings of the law (Matthew 15:9). In a similar vein, we might lament that we diligently prepare the instruments used in our own affairs, yet when it comes to sanctified matters, we display as much carelessness as we do in understanding God's commandments. This discrepancy in reverence becomes apparent when comparing our care for things that concern us with our care for matters pertaining to God.

Stepping away from the presence of God and focusing on our own gain, we find great fruit awaiting us—a fruit so significant that the Early Church writers likened the mystery of the Supper to the tree of life in the Garden of Eden (1 Cor. 11:30). They even drew a parallel between the abuse of this mystery and the unlawful eating of that forbidden tree. Christ is seen as the tree of life, and partaking of Him grants life to those who partake. Consider this: if a mere touch of Christ's garment's hem brought about a miraculous healing, how much greater is the benefit of receiving Christ's body and blood? Assuming equal faith in both instances, the latter should bring forth far greater blessings. Yet, it seems few fully realize the extent of these blessings. In light of this, it becomes clear that all these benefits are lost without proper preparation. As one of the Fathers pointed out, those who approach the sacred elements unprepared do not find Christ; rather, they find only the napkin or clothes of Christ. Thus, their unpreparedness not only hinders their spiritual growth but also brings about punishment. This principle stems from Haggai's words: "If one that is unclean by a dead body touch any of these, shall it be unclean? And the priests answered and said, It shall be unclean," (Haggai 2:13). Therefore, the one who approaches the holy sacraments *unprepared* pollutes their nature for himself. Similarly, in the case of an unworthy reception of medicine, if a purgative meant to eliminate a particular humor fails, not only is the benefit lost, but the condition worsens and the humor increases. Likewise, if our minds remain impure and unprepared, these sacred elements not only remain *ineffective* but might even lead to further harm. Unworthy reception of the sacraments might bring temporal or eternal judgments upon us. This dual perspective—reverence for God and personal gain—highlights the necessity of proper preparation. Therefore, let us diligently prepare ourselves, as the success of matters within the Church depends on proper preparation.

For this reason, the holy men of old, our virtuous predecessors, were meticulous in preparing themselves before engaging in specific acts of worship. Before praying, they would offer short prayers, known as ejaculations. They would devote half a day before the Sabbath to prepare themselves for worship. If preparation was essential for individual acts, how much more crucial is it for the sacraments? Preparation is non-negotiable for approaching the sacraments. This *examination* is binding upon us, and its absence excludes four types of people. First, children who lack the necessary maturity for self-examination are excluded. Second, those devoid of understanding, judgment, and rationality, such as the foolish and mentally unstable, are also excluded. Third, individuals who possess rational faculties but lack knowledge of essential religious principles and the doctrine of the sacraments are barred. Finally, those who possess knowledge yet remain wicked, stubborn, and unrepentant, failing to examine themselves, are also deemed unfit and unworthy to partake in this sacred Table.

The subject of examination pertains to ourselves, not others, as the Apostle states: "Let every man examine himself." Just as everyone ensures their own meal is prepared properly, they should also ensure the sanctification of their own hearts. This spiritual sustenance surpasses even the heavenly manna, yet it can be spoiled by our own malice. Additionally, since our attention naturally fixes on a single publican in the church, the Apostle urges us to reflect inwardly during our examination, just as sunlight is dispersed in the air.

Regarding the method of examination, we must consider the word's nature and purpose. The term "examination" is borrowed from goldsmiths' practice, involving a testing of metals. Therefore, learned individuals suggest that we examine ourselves by applying goldsmith rules. However, this doesn't rely on the sound or echo metals produce (as even the best metals can deceive in this aspect). Instead, it involves the touchstone and furnace as means of *testing*. Yet, these methods might be better suited for evaluating one's life as a whole rather than this particular issue. Others, relating the bread and wine to food, draw parallels to physicians' practices. Just as a full body might need emptying, even if fullness arises from a good humor such as blood, similarly, full bodies with bad humors must be purged—much like phlegmatic bodies filled with moisture. The same applies to those who think they are righteous enough or laden with grave sins. Such individuals should abstain from partaking until they cleanse themselves of self-righteous delusions and wickedness. Nonetheless, considering the subsequent words, "For if we would judge ourselves, we should not be judged," and, "when we are judged, we are chastened of the Lord, that we should not be condemned with the world," it seems the Apostle alludes to a *judicial* examination before a judge. Despite its goldsmith origins, the term's usage stems from legal proceedings. Therefore, let us take this approach: in this trial, let us judge ourselves internally and inquire whether we partake worthily or unworthily. To be more precise, we should set up our own internal judgment seat and rigorously examine whether we partake worthily or not. To clarify, this type of examination follows a judicial process, much like a legal trial. It involves self-judgment, asking whether we are guilty or innocent, worthy or unworthy. This sort of examination may well be understood as judicial, as in the context of appearing before a judge. In this sense, the term may originate from goldsmith terminology but functions within a judicial framework.

In this examination, we should consider whether we possess faith. Since faith relates to truth, we are tested by the truth. As the truth itself attests, "Cursed is he that continueth not in all things written in the Law." To examine ourselves, we must evaluate our record of transgressions and assess them against the truth. Afterward, recognizing our unworthiness, we should seek righteousness in Christ. Those who find themselves condemned will find solace in the saying, "This is a faithful saying, and worthy of all acceptation, that Christ Jesus came into the world to save sinners." This concept of faith leads us to Christ's redemption, and those who value Christ's death will gladly offer anything to receive it. God requires one thing of us—kindness and tender-heartedness toward one another, forgiving each other as God forgave us. This duty is *vital*. God views it as crucial, and although a person might be eager to engage in direct worship of the Lord, God would rather leave this duty unfulfilled than neglecting our duty to our brethren. Love for others is so vital that God prefers it over immediate worship. In the parable of the debtor, we see this clearly. While the debt is initially God's concern, His language becomes severe when a servant treats a fellow servant harshly (Matthew 18:32). Thus, harboring enmity toward our brethren may actually offend God more than our transgressions against God. This concludes the preliminary examination.

Once a person has discovered their own unworthiness through proper examination, they are to undergo a *transformation*. Here, note a contrast with our usual eating habits. While in our regular meals, the food is assimilated into us and becomes part of our substance, in this case, it's different. In this spiritual nourishment, *we are transformed into it*, not the other way around. This is analogous to the nature of leaven, which does not become unleavened and meld into the meal; rather, the meal transforms and becomes leavened. Similarly, in this sacramental food, we are transformed into it. Therefore, following the Apostle's guidance to examine oneself, the process should *culminate* in eating and drinking, not abstinence. Those who believed they honored the sacrament through abstaining actually dishonored it, for the directive is to examine oneself and then eat, not abstain. The sacrament is misused both by refraining after examining oneself and by partaking unworthily.

The elements received are referred to as bread and wine. Their nature is elucidated in Psalm 104, where the roles of bread and wine in nourishing, strengthening, and comforting are outlined. "And wine that maketh glad the heart of man, and oil to make his face to shine, and bread which strengtheneth man's heart," (Psa.

104:15). The body of Christ, represented by the bread, should have a similar effect on the soul as bread does on the body. As per Holy Scripture, bread strengthens the body, so our souls are strengthened against sin through Christ. In Genesis, Abraham's servants' hearts were strengthened with bread from Melchizedek (Gen. 14). Similarly, the Paschal Lamb provided strength to its eaters. Christ calls us to partake so that we receive spiritual strength for a new life, enabling us to strive for righteousness as if our actions could secure heaven. Christ's body not only is enlivened but also serves to enliven us and sanctify us. Just as the body's humors correspond to the components of bread, so too does the soul receive nourishment that empowers us to work towards the kingdom of heaven.

Conversely, Christ's blood should work in our souls as wine does in our bodies. This effect of wine is articulated in Psalm 104 and more vividly in Proverbs 31, where wine is said to *comfort* those in the throes of death. Just as wine brings a sense of gladness to the body, spiritual comfort is similarly brought by the blood of Jesus Christ. We cannot achieve absolute righteousness, just like angels or things in the heavens, which are impure in God's sight. In this way, we must focus on the active and passive righteousness of Christ, and have Christ's blood sprinkled in our hearts. We work with the active parts of righteousness as if surpassing the righteousness of Pharisees and the most righteous people on earth. However, when it comes to living or dying by our righteousness before God, we should abandon the Old Testament and rely on the blood of the New Testament, granted through faith.

During the sacrament's act of eating and drinking, as practiced in the Church, we are commanded to lift our hearts to the Lord. This is akin to eagles soaring to heaven, meditating on the invisible, and recalling Christ's suffering in the breaking of the body and shedding of His blood. This meditation, empowered by the Holy Spirit, sends our faith soaring.

The principal purpose is to remember Christ's death, which He entrusted to us during His final moments with us. This should linger in our minds because the last words of a departing friend often leave deep impressions and emotions. Reading about Christ's death evokes some response, hearing about it elicits more, and meditating on it evokes even more. However, having a visible portrayal of Christ's crucifixion before our eyes moves us most. Christ chose this wisely to ensure we never forget Him. As a memorial to the salvation from the flood, God left a rainbow after the deluge. Similarly, when He supernaturally provided manna to the Israelites, a jar of it was preserved in the Ark as a reminder. Having been saved by Christ's blood from the flood of our sins, we have Baptism to recall it. Similarly, being sustained by the manna of Christ's body, we're commanded to use this mystery to perpetually remember it.

Now, when it comes to the union between Christ and us, just as we inherit nothing from Adam but that which brings death to us, it is essential that we are connected with someone who can bring light to us (Romans 5). The means for such a union is this sacrament. What greater union can there be than that between what nourishes and what is nourished? Although this union cannot be fully expressed through reason, it must be believed. Christ, by being born of Mary, has united our nature with Him. Every reprobate also has a form of union with Christ by taking on the shape of a man. However, the distinction lies here: if an arm joined to the body lacks life, sensation, and the benefits of vital spirits, it may be united, but it's not truly a part of the body. Similarly, the wicked, living without faith, lack a soul and seem insensible, like lifeless appendages. They are not true members of Christ. It's insufficient to merely be joined to Christ's flesh as relatives of Christ, who, when speaking of spiritual connection, pointed to those who received His word by faith.

Symbols aside, to a genuine recipient, Christ is truly given, along with all that belongs to Christ in the redemption. However, we should not only consider our union with Christ, but also our connection to those who are part of the same mystical body. It's an association of love, which is why this mystery is referred to as a Communion. Because our union with Christ does not benefit God—since a multitude of men united to Him wouldn't profit Him—He has delegated the benefit to others. Just as Christ is food and drink to us, we should also be spiritual nourishment for others. Whatever wisdom, holiness, or material possessions we have, we should use them for the benefit of the less knowledgeable, the less holy, and those in need, respectively. This way, we become members not only of the natural but also the mystical body of Christ.

There is another purpose too. Just as external things undergo many transformations before becoming good food, like wheat going through various stages before becoming good bread, Christ's flesh underwent various sufferings. Christ's blood, analogous to the grape at its best, was pressed out of His veins and experienced painful trials. Shouldn't we also suffer with Him? We cannot avenge ourselves on the Jews like Pontius Pilate or Caiaphas, who were no more responsible for Christ's crucifixion than the nails, the cross, or the hammer. It was our sins that crucified Him, and those individuals were mere agents. We should direct our anger towards our own sins, arraign them, crucify them, and bury them forever. This is how we avenge Christ's crucifixion, not by punishing those who played their part, but by *defeating* our own sins.

It's also good to examine ourselves afterward, as assessing the soil can give an idea of the crop it will yield. However, observing the actual fruits removes all doubt. Repentance, faith, and love are leading indicators of a changed heart, but this post-communion assessment provides more assurance. If we find that we now rejoice more in the Word, strive for righteousness with greater zeal, and have fewer sins than before, these are reassuring signs of a genuine heart.

Now, if someone claims that these preceding signs (beginning with repentance and ending with charity) and the subsequent ones are good things but still feels more disheartened than encouraged upon self-examination, I say this: even if someone possessed perfect repentance and faith, they still shouldn't partake with the saints. These mysteries were intended for those who lack, not for the perfect. Therefore, one should not be discouraged from participating here due to *imperfections*. The key is to do everything with sincerity if not perfection. While it's true that true repentance and faith are prerequisites, these mysteries are for those who have needs, and imperfect believers should not hesitate to partake.

It's true that self-examination might lead to the agony Christ felt, even sweating drops of blood. However, our cold repentance doesn't allow us to reach this extent. Christ's agony was brought on by an *inner* heat. Yet, because our nature cannot fully experience this, Christ's agony also *fulfilled* our imperfections. Christ's perfect suffering atoned not only for our sins but also for our *shortcomings in righteousness*. Therefore, even if our examination doesn't lead us to the first degree of sorrow, let it at least bring us to the second degree—

grieving that we cannot grieve more. If we reach this level of sincerity, it is enough.

Finally, for those who have truly prepared themselves, Hezekiah's prayers (2 Chronicles 30) apply, that the Lord may complete the measure of their righteousness and forgive their sins when their hearts are fully devoted to seeking Him. This concludes the discussion of self-examination before and after the Lord's Supper.

A Treatise on the Fear of God

"Who knoweth the power of thine anger? Even according to thy fear, so is thy wrath," (Psa. 90:11).

The manner of expression used by Moses in Psalm 90:11 strongly emphasizes the *scarcity* of those who genuinely fear God. He asks, "Who feareth, *etc.*," but the thing sought and inquired about is not known to the asker. This implies that Moses himself didn't find *many* who truly feared God. This type of phrasing is applicable to all matters of God because our understanding of them is limited. On the other hand, when it comes to evil things, there's no need for questions or inquiries as they are all too familiar to everyone, as we witness through daily experience.

If we consider the times from Moses to David, from David to Isaiah, from Isaiah to Christ, and from Christ to the present day, we'll find it controversial to locate individuals who truly fear God. Yet, it's undebatable that the opposite type abounds. This isn't a matter of not knowing people's hearts; even God, who searches hearts, acknowledges this, as Isaiah 59:4 states that no one calls for justice or contends for truth. And when God saw that no one stepped forward, He marveled at the absence of an intercessor. This excess of evil isn't just attributed to individuals, but entire eras. In Genesis 6:5, it's stated that the thoughts of men's hearts were *continually* evil, and Micah, later, goes on to affirm that evil pervaded the night, which is a metaphor for all times. Therefore, Moses depicted *all day*, Micah depicted *all night*, and we might assert that *all time* is laden with evil. As for goodness, if we have any, it's a matter of intention, not practice; it's reserved for the future, not the present. Therefore, the prophet remarks that even birds of the air know their times, but we struggle to find the right time for virtuous deeds.

Furthermore, this excess of evil is evident not only in people but in places and actions. Heaven itself wasn't spared wickedness, as witnessed by the fall of the wicked angels. Even Paradise wasn't exempt. The Temple was marred by hypocrisy, and the number of evil actions grew. In light of this, David's outcry becomes significant, "Who understands his errors?" (Psalm 19:12). Our days are countable, but our sins are beyond numbering, compared to the sands of the sea. Considering individuals, times, places, and deeds, it's evident that few do good. Hence, the godly's lament and query about the scarcity of those who fear God.

The lesson we draw from this is that if we encounter offenses or causes for grief, we're witnessing nothing new; Moses, David, Isaiah, and even Christ encountered similar situations. Therefore, we can find solace in comparing our peaceful times with their times of affliction. Luther, addressing the question "Who feareth?" (Psalm 90), suggests that *no one fears before experiencing affliction*. This highlights affliction as a catalyst for true fear. This sense of fear should lead us to ask, "Lord, what shall I do?" or to echo David by asking, "What shall I repay unto the Lord?"

God's lament about the scarcity of those who fear Him should encourage us to lessen that complaint's validity by becoming genuine worshippers. At least one true worshipper, like Joshua, Caleb, Simeon, or Anna, can counterbalance this complaint. Achieving this would render the question void. However, it's worth noting that the inheritance of sins is hereditary, whereas the knowledge and fear of God aren't inherited, making them *rare* commodities.

Therefore, there's ample reason to fear. It's an irrevocable decree that we must all die (Hebrews 9), and Job claims life is short. However, we're well aware that all kinds of people have gone before us: wise men, pleasure-seekers, patriarchs, and prophets. We continually lose friends to the grave. We frequently pass over graves as we attend congregations. Death is a common certainty, yet the servants of God bemoan our ignorance of God's wrath. This ignorance is substantiated by Moses (Psalm 90), he prays to be *taught* about it. If we already knew this perfectly, his prayer would be unnecessary. Furthermore, he argues that because there's no fear, there's no understanding of God's wrath, illustrating the connection between lack of fear and lack of faith in this regard. Our lack of fear stems from a lack of persuasion about God's wrath. We don't fear things we don't consider evil, similar to how we don't readily approach things we fear, such as fire or water. Similarly, if we truly believed in God's wrath, we would fear it. Our ignorance of God's wrath is evident even though we partly understand it.

In natural matters, we're hesitant to face feared things and unafraid of things we don't perceive as evil. This principle applies to supernatural matters even more so. Thus, while we may have some understanding of God's wrath, we haven't fully grasped it as required.

Up until now, we need to comprehend that it's distinct when humans assess knowledge and when God judges it. Just as Isaiah differentiated between our estimation of fasting and God's evaluation of it (Isaiah 58), in the sense that we might consider someone abstaining from food to be a devout faster, yet the Lord's judgment may differ. Similarly, we can distinguish between how we value knowledge in our eyes versus how the Lord values it. It's insufficient to claim, "I've quoted this," or "I've read that," or "I've spoken about this," and consequently assert *knowledge*. This holds no sway in God's assessment. Just as the Lord determines the true nature of fasting, He also assesses the knowledge of those who surpass the ancient Jewish Rabbis and exceed the wise men of the pagans. This isn't surprising, as just as there's a type of wise ignorance and learned inexperience, there's also an ignorant knowledge, a foolish kind of wisdom that has spread across the world. To clarify, let's draw from Isaiah 6:9, a passage frequently quoted in the New Testament

(Matthew 13, Acts 28, and Romans 11). Here we learn that there can be a *seeing* without *truly seeing*, a form of hearing that doesn't genuinely listen. Similarly, one can possess knowledge without it truly being knowledge before God. This occurs because the Lord doesn't recognize knowledge that lacks practical application. Even if we have extensive knowledge but fail to put it into practice, it holds no significance in God's view. Just as God assesses knowledge in this manner, so do we; if we've strived to impart precept upon precept and yet the recipient hasn't profited, despite appearing attentive, we consider and accuse them as someone who didn't hear at all.

It's more beneficial to have no light than to hide a candle under a basket, as God doesn't consider *concealed light* as light. Having the ears of an idol is as good as having no ears, for such ears don't *truly* hear. Similarly, knowledge detached from practice isn't genuine knowledge. When we mistakenly believe we possess great knowledge due to hearing numerous sermons, we must erase many of those sermons from our count if we haven't acted upon them. In God's perspective, such sermons are meaningless to us. We often assert that the absence of means signifies God's curse, and there's truth in this; however, if a unique blessing isn't capitalized upon, it results in a unique judgment when abused. A place where such unique blessings were wasted faces a more significant judgment than a place without these blessings, for it's worse to have heard much yet gained no profit from it. As David wisely said, "It is good for me that I have been afflicted; that I might learn thy statutes," (Psalm 119:71). This statement holds true for him, yet affliction doesn't yield goodness for everyone; some become worse due to it, like Lot's wife who turned into a pillar of salt.

Two factors hinder the maturation of knowledge. Firstly, people proudly *remain ignorant*, falsely convincing themselves that they know what they actually don't (self-flattery). Secondly, there's a hardness of heart that prevents true benefit from knowledge. Either people presume deep knowledge or they become unfeeling and hardened. If God's judgments are spoken, they're not feared; if His promises are offered, there's no rejoicing. Essentially, whatever is said fails to move them. Even if vast knowledge is poured into such a heart, it amounts to nothing.

As we're reluctant to perceive God's wrath as it is, we recognize it in terms of justice. The concept of God's wrath signifies justice to us. While other qualities of God might not stir us, His wrath does. Emotions are typically roused by their objects; for instance, fear arises from wrath. If we fear the anger of a person, especially a ruler, considering how immense a prince's wrath seems to us, what then of God's wrath? We will undoubtedly encounter it one way or another, either to endure it or to reconcile with God and avoid it. Therefore, to disclose this wrath, Moses teaches us to see our sin and to subject us to *the law's confines* and its prescribed penalties.

This helps us value the mercy offered in Christ even more. The reason we fail to appreciate mercy is because we lightly regard our sins. We underestimate our sin because we fail to revere God's wrath against it. Our estimation of peace is akin to our estimation of war, and we value abundance in the same way we value scarcity. To gain a true understanding of abundance, we can look at the famine in Samaria or Edom, where donkey heads were sold at a high price. Through such experiences, we can rightly assess abundance. In times of affliction, we're directed to focus on God's wrath, which is the cause of our suffering. We shouldn't remain stuck in affliction but keep our gaze on our sin. Without recognizing our sin, we may either grumble against God's judgments like Jonah or end up cursing the day of our birth like Job. In such cases, we fail to benefit from our affliction.

Therefore, our inability to derive benefit from adversity stems from our lack of understanding of its causes. We remain fixated on the effects, lamenting the actions themselves without delving into the cause and origin. Consider when a person faces adversity due to the actions of a wicked individual; they become incensed with that person rather than turning their gaze towards God. This is akin to quarreling with the staff used to strike us while disregarding the striker. Essentially, people focus on the blow without addressing the devil's instigation behind it. Just as we examine the devil's motives, we should scrutinize God's visitations. Often, we vent our anger on the punishment while neglecting to humble ourselves before the one who wields the punishment. But what do we achieve with this approach? Even if we were to wrest the punishment from God's grasp, what advantage would it be if He proceeds to wield a sword, a mallet, or a massive rock to not just strike us, but to shatter us into fragments? It's wise not to contest the effect but to confront the cause. Now, two factors blind us from seeing God's wrath in our afflictions. First, since we aren't immediately consumed by God's anger, we brush aside any suspicion that He's displeased with us. We fail to acknowledge His wrath until it strikes like a harbinger of death. Some perish suddenly from strokes, while others gradually waste away from lingering illnesses. This is more perilous as it's less noticeable and ends up killing us rather than forewarning us. The second reason is that just as God's judgments can be perceived as mercies and expressions of His love, many of His mercies are delivered through judgments and are manifestations of His wrath. Jeremiah notes that the Lord allowed Josiah to reign in wrath over His people, even though Josiah was a righteous king. The takeaway from this is that God's anger operates within Him, much like all other emotions when they haven't found expression in us. This is why, since we don't disapprove of our sins, God disapproves of us; because we don't dislike our corruptions, He shows His disapproval of them; and because we're not angry with ourselves, God becomes angry with us. Sin deserves wrath, and *either* we administer that wrath to ourselves, or the Lord administers it to us. If we express anger towards ourselves and take offense at our actions, as in 2 Corinthians 7, the Lord will alleviate His wrath; if we judge ourselves, God won't judge us.

If at any point we consider God's wrath, we view it as powerless. Wrath is effective; even the wrath of a lesser being can prompt action. I wish we feared the Lord's wrath as much as we do a prince's anger. Yet we regard God's wrath as we do His mercy, perceiving Him as possessing feeble anger and limited power. We thank Him for His mercies as if He were a stingy and reluctant giver. When we perform our duties towards God, we approach Him cautiously, measuring our actions as if we are striking a deal with Him. Yet when it comes to our wickedness, we exhibit boldness and extravagance. We behave as if God were either blind and oblivious to our actions or as if His arms were restrained from striking us. However, the weakness of God surpasses the greatest strength of humans. Even God's weakness is mightier than human strength. If we conceive of this weakness, it's comparable to the touch of a person's little finger. If we approach God's little finger and consider the confession of all the wise men in Egypt, including their magicians, we'll realize that in the extraordinary plagues that befell the land, they recognized the finger of the Lord at work. In Job's afflictions, wherein he lost possessions, livestock, and children, the devil referred to it as a mere touch of God's little finger, yet it brought complete devastation. The breath in a person is considered frail, but the Lord's very breath renders everything in a person like grass and their finest qualities like the flower of the grass when the Lord's breath blows upon it (Isaiah 40:17, Psalm 18:8). Smoke emanates from His nostrils, and a consuming fire emerges from His mouth (Psalm 18:8). This emphasizes the potency of His nostrils, underscoring the might within His wrath's frailty. If this is God's weakness, then His strength—when compared to a giant or a lion, the mightiest of beasts—is truly formidable. If He's so powerful that a mere touch of His finger can impact us, how terrifying must He be when His arm strikes us? What then when He approaches with His armament—a sharpened sword and a drawn bow, ready for battle? Whether we're distant or near, His bow is poised to reach us, His sword is ready to strike. Yet beyond swords and bows, He has legions of creatures under His command—fire, hail, thunderbolts, and even the lowliest creatures like lice and flies—to be unleashed upon us. Thus, if the sword doesn't find us, the thunderbolt will; if hail doesn't finish us, fire will consume us; if fire fails to burn, the mallet will crush us. Furthermore, He commands chariots and thousands of chariots within whirlwinds, and pillars of fire to terrify us. More significantly, He has thousands and twenty thousands of angels at His beck and call to wreak havoc. The wrath of the Almighty is vast; His power never falters. All His creations serve Him. When one has completed their task, another takes over. Thus, we will surely grow weary of enduring before He grows weary of afflicting, or before His capacity for punishment diminishes. But beyond contemplating His strength, let's consider our own weakness. We're as fragile as pottery vessels; a mere collision shatters us, reducing us to shards with every impact. If the Lord raises His rod against us, we're reduced to dust. If a small rod proves inadequate, He'll employ an iron crowbar to shatter us. In short, the Lion walks before Him; the Unicorn serves Him. Behemoth is conquered by His sword; Leviathan cannot withstand Him. The difference between God's power and that of princes is immense. Princes can only seize the body, and their wrath extends only to this life. However, God seizes both body and soul; His anger remains as intense, if not more so, in the afterlife.

Our understanding should culminate in fear. It's evident that ignorance is audacious, while experience should naturally evoke apprehension for imminent or present events. Moses found this concept so perplexing that he concluded that lacking fear indicates ignorance (Psalm 90). This is unsurprising as the Holy Spirit frequently links fear and divine wisdom, either as its origin or its culmination. The commencement of wisdom is plainly in fear (Proverbs 1), and its ultimate fulfillment is evident (Ecclesiastes 12). True wisdom is unattainable without this starting point, and perfection remains elusive without this conclusion. The reasons we often lack fear are twofold: either because we possess an inflated sense of our own wisdom or because our hearts are unyielding. Both of these maladies are remedied through fear. The first is substantiated in Proverbs 21, where it's written: "Blessed is the man that feareth: but he that hardneth his heart shall fall into evil." Here, fear of God stands in stark contrast to hardness of heart. The second is demonstrated in Proverbs 3:7, "Be not wise in thine own eyes, but fear the Lord." Fear of God serves as a corrective to our self-conceit. In essence, those who lack fear possess either pride or callousness. With either of these two, there's no room for wisdom, and consequently, such individuals lack genuine knowledge. Fear and wisdom are inseparable; they're the conclusion and embodiment of all love. The rationale is that love becomes complacent without fear, and complacency leads to estrangement from one's beloved, as seen in the Song of Solomon, where the Church laments losing her Love while she slumbers. Thus, just as fear marks the beginning, fear also marks the potential loss. In Hebrews 12, after addressing love, the Apostle injects a tremulous note, closing with the fiery assertion that "God is a consuming fire."

Since the time of Adam's sin, all are predisposed to fear and to seek refuge. This is the reason why a thief trembles in the presence of a judge, or why a dead tree evokes a fear in the superstitious worshipper's conscience. Even the devil trembles, and each sinner, when they shun fear after sinning, essentially justifies the devil in this regard. By shrugging off the premonition of divine judgment, they plunge further into wickedness, whether within the Church, outside of it, or even in hell itself.

Our fear shouldn't be indiscriminate; it must be of a certain quality. As Abraham proclaimed in Genesis, if the fear of God were absent, then there would be no place for God's Church. Thankfully, due to God's mercy, we haven't reached such a state. While the present-day Church isn't as blameless as it should be—in fact, it's often condemnable when compared to its ideal state—we're not at a point where there's no fear of God among us. However, we do fall short in this regard; our knowledge of God and fear of Him doesn't measure up to our teaching and the justice of God. When we consider our constant teaching in comparison to our intermittent progress in learning, and when we observe the signs of God's judgments manifest in the neighboring nations, we realize our fear is inadequate and our knowledge limited. The Lord might bring a case against us due to our insufficient fear that, although present, lacks proportion.

Thus, just as meditations on the law must exceed mere musings and be infused with strength and comfort that surpass all worldly thoughts, and just as God demands not just hearing but the kind of attentive listening where nothing else occupies our mind as intently and cautiously, we must also fear and do so in accordance with the circumstance. This congruence, or lack thereof, will ultimately condemn us, for our emotions aren't aligned with their rightful objects. However, an even greater predicament emerges—just as we fail to elevate our affections sufficiently for good things, we overextend them for evil things. We *don't* fear God enough, we fear the world too much, we love God's word too sparingly, and we cherish our worldly gains too excessively. Thus, a discord exists within us; our fear for spiritual matters is lacking, while our fear for worldly matters is excessive.

Undoubtedly, if we could extend this kind of fervor towards the loftiest pursuits as we do for the lesser, it would greatly vindicate us. However, because we dread lesser matters to such an extent and revere greater matters so lightly, this will indeed be our indictment. Furthermore, our fear doesn't match the gravity of God's wrath, as evidenced by our usual minimal and inadequate approach. The Word itself establishes the fear of God as the measure for both fearing and forsaking sin (Job 1). However, when we diminish the weight of our fear of God, our departure from evil also becomes insubstantial.

In this way, we observe that God requires order. First, we should provide for His kingdom, and only then attend to other matters. But when we undermine the primacy of God's fear, we bolster His accusations against us.

FINIS

A Treatise on the Resurrection

Psalm 16:10: "For thou wilt not leave my soul in the grave; neither wilt thou suffer thine holy one to see corruption."

Philippians 3:20, "For our conversation is in heaven; from whence also we look for the Saviour, the Lord Jesus Christ: who shall change our vile body, that it may be fashioned like unto his glorious body, according to the working whereby he is able even to subdue all things unto himself."

Do we share the conviction of the Psalmist, who assures us that we shall rise and escape corruption? That death is a slumber, the grave a bed? That the same God who daily raises the sun from its hiding place will also lift us from the earth? If so, then we possess true faith, a faith that can be fortified by preoccupying ourselves with the contemplation of death long before it arrives. Many individuals, by delaying their thoughts on death until the very end, perish with a heathen-like attitude. Others, wishing to appear valiant, welcome death unnaturally, not because they are burdened by their own corruption and transgressions, but because, like animals, they neither rejoice in heavenly matters nor dread the pains of hell. These individuals, displaying less wakefulness and sense than animals, are more lethargic and unfeeling than those who are reluctant to depart.

Yet, even the latter, who demonstrate a more natural disposition and some semblance of conscience, deviate from nature, rendering themselves more monstrous and perilous. Although the common populace praises this form of death—asserting that the individual passed away as gently as a lamb or as a bird emerges from its shell—truthfully, they might declare that such a death is beastly. The dying person does not exhibit repentance, confession of sin, demonstration of faith in salvation through Christ, or affirmation of hope in a joyful resurrection and transition to eternal life. This inclination toward extremes—either excessive fear of death or insufficient fear—reveals our nature.

To alleviate excessive fear, we can turn to this remedy: "My flesh doth rest in hope, for thou wilt not leave my soul in the grave," (Psalm 16:10). Some individuals may also calmly embrace death, reasoning that they willingly surrender what they owe by necessity. They consider death a debt owed to God and are content to pay it, be it sooner or later. The perspective of God's children, however, differs significantly. They derive greater benefit from death than any others, yet having tasted the blessings of the land of the living even in this life, they remain unsatisfied until they reach fullness. Such believers, departing in their maturity and fullness of days, are gathered in their appointed time into the Lord's barn like sheaves of wheat. Having waged a valiant battle, completed their race, and upheld a steadfast faith, they joyfully await the crown of glory prepared for them. Meditating on death, therefore, is beneficial. We are reminded of our mortality as we witness others around us passing away. Numerous individuals of the same age and disposition, breathing the same air and consuming the same sustenance as us, precede us in departing this world. They are spared the calamities that our prolonged neglect of God's word threatens to bring upon us. Let us strive to entrust our flesh to hope, so that our transition from this life may resemble a voyage across the sea, the labor of a woman giving birth, an escape from prison, or a return from exile.

It is not my intention to encourage hastening one's death or to suggest reading this text with an eye to hastening one's deliverance. Instead, we should learn to *respond* when God signals for us to depart, *ready* to move in faith and hope in His promises, having a deep awareness that our sins are forgiven, a firm belief in God's power to raise us, and an unwavering expectation of an even more glorious existence beyond this life. By doing so, we will *rest* in God's hands. When our physical faculties wane, we shall leave this world calmly and at an appropriate time, voluntarily shedding the earthly vessel rather than being forcibly torn from it. The unwise desire for untimely death either stems from lowly minds or from individuals whose spirits are already dead within their bodies. The victory of the righteous emerges from their unwavering assurance that the same God who resurrects them each morning will resurrect them on the final day. Just as He raised Christ, their head, He will also raise them, His members. This conviction soothes the flesh, dispelling any trembling that prevents many from drinking the cup that the Lord has prepared for them.

In this era, the doctrine of resurrection is particularly pertinent. Wicked heretics attempt to deprive us of the comfort it offers. When faced with temptation, whether from the devil directly or through his agents, responding in vague faith, such as resting in our implicit faith in the Papist creed or stating that we believe as the Church believes, is inadequate. Instead, we must possess an understanding of the resurrection that cannot be shaken. Satan cunningly arranges for adversaries who appear to agree with us in doctrine yet subtly deny the power of the resurrection. These opponents might acknowledge the concept of resurrection, but either insist that it's already happened or play games with its significance.

Once again, should we assume that the Sadducees universally opposed the doctrine of resurrection? Not at all. They had their false interpretations and contrived explanations, guided by Satan's cunning strategy to maintain what he intended to undermine. Even philosophers had eloquent speeches on the immortality of the soul. However, when it came to the matter of the bodily resurrection, they found it ridiculous and implausible. This sentiment was so strong that Epicureans and Stoics ridiculed Paul's discourse on the resurrection from the dead (Acts 17:18). In response, some mocked him, while others said they would hear him later on the matter. If the resurrection were merely about renewing the mind, as some mistakenly believe, then the Academics and followers of Plato might have embraced this doctrine. Yet, the stumbling block for them is the revival of the *natural* body, which, after being consumed by air, fire, water, or earth, is to be restored with *supernatural* attributes. Just as philosophers and heretics find this teaching intolerable, few common believers genuinely receive it as evidenced by their lives.

Moreover, a more dangerous evil lurks. Through Satan's cunning, this mystery of iniquity is insidiously implanted in the minds of the educated, leading them to debate certain passages of the Old Testament that godly, learned, and ancient Fathers have interpreted as referring to the resurrection. These interpretations are rejected by these individuals. Examples include Job 19:25-27, Isaiah 26:19, and Daniel 12:2. Although it may not have been their intention to misconstrue these passages, Satan's crafty scheme was to misuse the truth and weaken our faith. God allowed Satan to buffet them to a certain extent. To be better equipped for the day of trial and stand firmly in times of temptation, we will rely on God's help to present explicit testimonies from the Scriptures that support this doctrine. Additionally, we will cite passages that imply this concept even if they do not explicitly affirm it. Subsequently, we will unveil the deceptive guise of heretics, through which they attempt to win support for their beliefs. To better counter the devil and his followers, let's first examine the account of Enoch's translation in Genesis 5:24. The Fathers of old have recognized a clear testimony of resurrection in this passage, and while I partly agree with them, I differ in one aspect. I cannot assert, as they did, that Enoch's body is in heaven since, to date, only Christ has risen from the dead and become the *firstfruits* of those who have fallen asleep. Although Enoch and Elijah did not experience death as other Fathers did, Hebrews 11:39 indicates that the Fathers of old, including Enoch, did *not* receive the promise in its fullness. Therefore, Enoch's flesh cannot yet be in heaven. While Enoch's departure occurred through unknown means, it is certain that the same God who concealed Moses' body from even the devil's searching eyes could also hide the bodies of Enoch and Elijah. The Lord possesses infinite ways of concealment and incomprehensible means of discovery for both Enoch's and Moses' bodies.

Additionally, in Hebrews 11:35, it is mentioned that they suffered to obtain a better resurrection, implying the resurrection of the flesh. Moreover, Exodus 3:6 records God's words to Moses, "I am the God of thy fathers, the God of Isaac, and the God of Jacob." Although this passage may seem inadequate to support such a weighty matter, Christ Himself uses it as a shield against the Sadducees in Matthew 22:32. In this context, Christ infers from these words, "God is not the God of the dead, but of the living." This underscores that Abraham, Isaac, and Jacob are alive, with their bodies kept by the Lord as well as their souls. As both the prophets and Christ Himself have employed this passage for this purpose, we too can safely use it as evidence for the resurrection.

Furthermore, it is also written in Job 19:25-27: "I know that my Redeemer liveth, and he shall stand the last on the earth. And though after my skin, worms destroy this body, yet in my flesh I shall see God, whom I shall see for myself, and my eyes shall behold, and not another; though my reins are consumed within me." Even the heretics begrudgingly concede this to some extent, though with a perverse intention, interpreting it as a rising unto sanctification within this life. There are others of more respectable judgment who expound this as a renewal and restoration of his flesh to health and vigor after it was afflicted with sores and plagued with ulcers. But, supposing this were the case, which is indeed an untenable interpretation, how could he have believed such a thing? Instead, being persuaded that God, who could restore vitality to his body when only partly afflicted by corruption, could much more revitalize it while corruption was still minor? This confidence stemmed from hope in God's power, as displayed in Ezekiel 37:5-6, where a significant type of resurrection is portrayed: "Thus says the Lord God to these bones: Behold, I will cause breath to enter into you, and you shall live. And I will lay sinews upon you, and will cause flesh to come upon you, and cover you with skin, and put breath in you, and you shall live, and you shall know that I am the Lord."

While the chief intention of the Holy Spirit is to foreshadow the restoration of the people from captivity, this is skillfully portrayed under the remarkable figure of the resurrection and renewal of the flesh on the last day. Thus, the passage conveys the message that just as herbs appear dead in winter but sprout anew in spring due to the life-giving sap concealed within their roots, and just as the bodies of the faithful seem to perish when they are interred in the earth but shall rise again through the seed given in Christ, so the Israelites, who appeared to wither and perish in their exile, shall be restored to their homeland and granted freedom. This portrayal is indicated by the phrase "even with this body shall they rise." An equally significant passage is found in Daniel 12:2, "And many of them that sleep in the dust of the earth shall awake, some to everlasting life, and some to shame and everlasting contempt." This aligns with Christ's words in John 5:28-29, "Marvel not at this: for the hour is coming, in which all that are in the graves shall hear his voice. And shall come forth, they that have done good, unto the resurrection of life; and they that have done evil, unto the resurrection of damnation."

When we recognize the clarity of the doctrine of faith presented in the New Testament regarding resurrection and the fact that there is no *new* teaching therein that does not find its roots in the Old Testament, we can conclude that the doctrine of resurrection is indeed validated in the Old Testament. Among numerous passages, our current Psalm is a significant one, where it states, "Thou wilt not leave my soul in the grave, nor suffer thine holy one to see corruption." The reference to "soul" should be understood as his entire being, in the sense used in 1 Corinthians 15:45, where the Apostle refers to Genesis 2:7 and says, "The first man Adam was made a living soul: and the last Adam was made a quickening spirit." The reason for his assertion of bodily resurrection is drawn from the power of our Savior Christ, referred to as "Thou wilt not suffer thine holy one to see corruption." This interpretation is affirmed by both Peter in Acts 2 and Paul in Acts 23. The Apostle Paul clarifies that David did not speak these words about himself, as he experienced corruption upon his death, but rather about Christ, in whom no corruption dwells. Thus, as a member of Christ, David foresaw by faith that a Holy One would arise from his loins, having the power to raise not only His own body without corruption but also the bodies of others from corruption. This is elaborated further in Philippians 3:20-21: "Our conversation is in heaven, from whence also we look for the Saviour, even the Lord Jesus Christ: who shall change our vile body, that it may be fashioned like unto his glorious body, according to the working whereby he is able even to subdue all things unto himself."

With regard to the places of the Old Testament, let's now turn our attention to those in the New Testament. Firstly, let us reflect on the words with which Jesus confounded the Sadducees in Matthew 22:32: "I am the God of Abraham, and the God of Isaac, and the God of Jacob." God cannot be called the God of Abraham if he remains dead, unless his body is raised, as well as his soul. This distinction is vital since it doesn't say, "I am the God of Abraham's soul," but rather, "I am the God of *Abraham*." Thus, Abraham's bodily resurrection is necessitated. In Matthew 25:31, Jesus states, "When the Son of man shall come in his glory, and all the holy angels with him, then shall he sit upon the throne of his glory." Similarly, in Luke 14:13-14, Jesus teaches, "But when thou makest a feast, call the poor, the maimed, the lame, the blind: and thou shalt be blessed; for they cannot recompense thee: for thou shalt be recompensed at the resurrection of the just." Here, Jesus implies that though temporal sacrifices may seem in vain, they will be recompensed at the resurrection of the righteous.

In John 5:28-29, the Lord reveals the resurrection of both the righteous and wicked, urging us not to marvel that our souls are raised to life since He can raise our bodies from death: "Marvel not at this: for the hour is coming, in the which all that are in the graves shall hear his voice. And shall come forth, they that have done good, unto the resurrection of life; and they that have done evil, unto the resurrection of damnation."

Likewise, Martha's faith in resurrection is evident in John 11, as previously mentioned. In Acts 3:19, the Apostle Peter calls the resurrection a time of refreshing, a comforting idea analogous to how a weary traveler seeks rest at an inn. In Acts 4:15, Paul professes his faith in the resurrection of both the just and unjust. Additionally, 1 Corinthians 15 thoroughly addresses and confirms this doctrine. Similarly, 2 Corinthians 5:10 speaks of standing before the judgment seat of Christ to receive recompense for our deeds. In Philippians 3:21, the transformation of our bodies is presented.

In 1 Thessalonians 4:14-17, the manner and culmination of resurrection are described, "For if we believe that Jesus died and rose again, even so them also which sleep in Jesus will God bring with him. For this we say unto you by the word of the Lord, that we which are alive and remain unto the coming of the Lord shall not prevent them which are asleep. For the Lord himself shall descend from heaven with a shout, with the voice of the archangel, and with the trump of God: and the dead in Christ shall rise first: then we which are alive and remain shall be caught up together with them in the clouds, to meet the Lord in the air: and so shall we ever be with the Lord."

Moreover, Hebrews 11 showcases the saints' endurance of martyrdom for the prospect of a superior resurrection. Verse 35 explains that they suffered to receive a better resurrection. Similarly, verse 39 declares that these saints didn't fully receive the promise, awaiting the last member of Christ to be ready for their fulfillment. Notably, 2 Peter 3:10 and Revelation 20:11-13 emphasize the profound transformation of the universe and the final judgment, affirming the resurrection's significance.

Now, as we have received the truth of this *doctrine*, let's consider further into it through reason. On one hand, we cannot deny the reality of resurrection, for the scriptures confirm it; to deny it would require forsaking our faith and rejecting the scriptures. On the other hand, when we examine these matters more closely, we find that reason also supports resurrection; to oppose it with reason would be foolish. The reasons we'll present are drawn from God himself, from the natural order, the creatures, the benefits associated with the truth of this doctrine, and the disadvantages that arise from denying it.

The arguments rooted in the nature of God are derived from His own attributes, both in His intrinsic nature and in His role as a Mediator within the Trinity. Within His intrinsic nature, we must consider His truth, justice, and power. His truth is steadfast, as His promises in Christ Jesus are always "Yes" and "Amen," thus whatever He has declared in His word must be believed, even if external circumstances appear contrary. His justice is inseparable from His truth; it demands the fulfillment of His promises in rewarding the righteous and the execution of His threats in punishing the ungodly. For instance, in Matthew 25:33,

Jesus distinguishes between sheep and goats according to righteous judgment. Likewise, in Luke 16:23, the rich man is tormented in hell while Lazarus is comforted in Abraham's bosom, illustrating the *just* nature of divine judgment. Another pertinent example is found in 2 Thessalonians 1:6-7, where God's righteous retribution for persecution is emphasized.

Furthermore, God's justice necessitates that the wicked, who have dishonored Him and misused their bodies for sin, should experience both spiritual and bodily punishment. Conversely, the righteous, whose bodies were instruments of God's glory, should experience the fullness of His promises. This symmetry of justice underscores that the righteous receive rewards and the wicked face torments. This is further demonstrated through the lives of patriarchs, prophets, apostles, martyrs, and believers who suffered in this life while awaiting heavenly recompense. The wicked, however, may prosper in this world, but this is temporary; divine justice demands eternal punishment for their unrepentant sins. Thus, God's justice, linked with His truth, makes it inevitable that the righteous rise to heavenly joy while the wicked rise to hellish torment.

Moreover, the doctrine of resurrection is also supported by the omnipotence of God. The power that created the universe from nothing is certainly capable of renewing the flesh from the earth, just as it once formed Adam from dust. Renewing a body from bones is no more challenging than creating a body from a single bone. God's power can restore flesh, bones, and sinews, and beautify them with skin, just as it originally created them. This power is as evident in the restoration of the body as it is in its dissolution. If God can transform flesh to corruption, corruption to worms, and worms to dust, then surely, He can reverse this process, bringing dust back to worms, worms back to putrefaction, and ultimately restoring the body to immortality.

In our *Confession*, we acknowledge God's almighty nature at the very outset, and this is not without reason. His mercy and justice are effective because of His power, enabling Him to fulfill promises and execute judgments. When we assert God's almightiness, we affirm that He can accomplish whatever He wills. While God cannot lie, this does not diminish His omnipotence any more than stating a mighty leader cannot be defeated diminishes their valor. God's power is manifest in creation, providence, and preservation. Creation illustrates His ability to bring order from *nothingness*, and the same power can restore flesh from *decay*. In short, God's omnipotence assures us that resurrection is entirely plausible and harmonious with His nature and attributes.

The providence of God teaches us this truth, whether we consider it in the natural course of events or in the governance of His Church. In the realm of nature, the Prophet Isaiah declares, "Awake and sing, ye that dwell in the dust: for the dew is as the dew of herbs, and the earth shall cast out her dead," (Isaiah 26:19). This passage signifies that the same God who caused Aaron's staff to blossom and brings vibrant colors from lifeless flowers and flourishing branches from withered herbs is fully capable of raising us in our bodies to the brilliance of His glory, even if we have been laid in the filth of the dust. Similarly, in 1 Corinthians 15:35-38, the Apostle Paul addresses doubts about resurrection. He uses the analogy of sowing seeds, comparing it to the resurrection of the dead, and emphasizes that God gives a body as He pleases to every seed. Paul rebukes those who question this truth, asserting that God's power can indeed accomplish such feats.

Moreover, the ability of God to raise the dead is evident in both the course of nature and His dealings with the Church. God's intervention in the course of nature is witnessed in the miraculous births of Isaac and Jesus. The former was born to Abraham and Sarah when nature seemed to have failed, and the latter was born of the Virgin Mary, who had not known a man. If God could fulfill His promises in these extraordinary ways, raising us from the dry earth is well within His power. Consider the faith of Abraham as he was willing to sacrifice Isaac, believing that God could raise him even from the dead (Hebrews 11:19).

Furthermore, the providence of God in His Church offers additional confirmation. Reflect on how God multiplied His people despite natural odds, as seen in Abraham and Sarah's bearing a child, and in David's lineage leading to the birth of Jesus. God's guidance and preservation of His people, such as their passage through the Red Sea and their sustenance in the wilderness, serve as reminders of His capability. The Shunammite's son being raised by Elisha, the dead man revived by touching Elisha's bones, and the deliverance of Daniel, Shadrach, Meshach, Abednego, and Jonah in extraordinary circumstances all attest to God's power over life and death.

Furthermore, the events after Christ's crucifixion, where graves opened and saints arose, manifest God's power. All these instances, when scrutinized, underscore the might of God's providence over life and death. The angels' appearances in human form, as well as the rising of the dead before and after Christ's resurrection, illustrate the timing and purposes of God's providence.

In summary, the providence of God, as demonstrated in both nature and His dealings with His Church, completely supports the doctrine of resurrection. The same God who commands nature, raises the dead, and orchestrates miraculous events, can certainly raise our bodies from the earth. The evidence is resounding—God's power knows no bounds, and our faith in the resurrection is well-founded.

Now let's examine the reasons drawn from God as our Mediator. We'll consider certain actions performed in His own person, as well as aspects to be observed in the means that lead us to Him. In Luke 8:55,

Jesus resurrected the daughter of Jairus from death to life. A more remarkable case is found in Luke 7:14, where He revived a widow's son lying on a bier, ready for burial. Even more astonishingly, in John 11:44, He raised Lazarus, who had been *dead* for four days. Lastly, in Matthew 26, Jesus mightily raised Himself after being dead for three days and nights, without any corruption. Who, then, can doubt, under the threat of damnation, that the same Jesus Christ can raise our mortal and corruptible bodies? Who can question His ability to transform our lowly bodies, making them like His glorious body, through His mighty power, by which He can subdue all things to Himself? Consider how Pilate sealed the stone covering Christ's burial place and set armed guards at the tomb. Yet, all their efforts couldn't prevent Jesus from rising.

Furthermore, Christ's resurrection was witnessed by Mary, several disciples, and over five hundred people, confirming that His rising was bodily, not merely spiritual. Just as He rose in flesh, so shall we rise. He didn't rise for His own sake; His pure birth, holy life, and innocent death were all for us. He sanctified, justified, and will glorify us. His suffering was both physical and spiritual, emphasizing that He redeemed both body and soul from guilt and punishment. His resurrection was bodily and spiritual, restoring holiness to both body and soul. His ascension, in body and soul, honors the glory of both, as He purchased them. Therefore, the resurrection of the flesh must inevitably follow. If we are united with Christ through faith, bone of His bones and partakers of His flesh, His bodily acts must extend to us. The word of God impacts both our bodies and souls, as our senses—eyes, ears, tongues—participate in its reception and response. Thus, the effects of God's word will manifest in both realms.

Likewise, in prayer, our souls and bodies are engaged; we lift our hands, kneel, elevate our eyes, cry out, and prostrate ourselves. This dual involvement is mirrored in the sacraments. Baptism, with its bodily actions of dipping and emergence, signifies our resurrection to grace for both body and soul. The Eucharist involves body and soul, where our eyes behold, ears hear, hands handle, mouths taste, and the soul believes. This is further evidence of the resurrection encompassing both aspects of our being.

Creation itself testifies to this truth. Angels and other creatures yearn for the day of the Son of God's revelation. Even demons fear it, as they pleaded with Jesus not to torment them prematurely. Disorder in creation implies restoration to order. Humanity especially awaits resurrection, as it holds manifold benefits and prevents dire consequences. The expectation of glorious resurrection enables patience in adversity, abstention from evil, and zealous pursuit of good. Without this hope, sanctification would lose meaning, sin would flourish, godliness would wane, and dishonor to God would abound. Resurrection is the culmination of God's promises, indispensable for both the godly and the wicked. Without it, the righteous would be unfortunate, and the wicked less miserable. Resurrection fosters worship and conscience in bodily conduct, and discourages sin.

FINIS

A Treatise on Hypocrisy

There are two essential aspects in Religion: substance and ceremony or façade. We possess *only* one of them. The first, to circumcise our hearts, making them bleed, is a remarkably challenging task. We tend to settle for hearing, as opinions often suffice for common people. They resemble children who, upon seeing a face in a mirror, believe it to be a person, discussing and addressing it. This superficial hearing may have had occasional benefits in the past, but as one has said, now it amounts to mere listening, eating, drinking, and talking. A mere display can move the multitude, as seen with Absalom. Although a beast, upon vowing and Jezebel proclaiming a fast, people followed them, thinking the Queen had become religious, and Absalom was worthy of a kingdom. Similarly, hypocrites deem just men. Reproving is a good man's duty, as under the law, the accuser used to cast the first stone. The thief on the cross stated, "Darest thou reprove, being in the same condemnation?" This illustrates a case of premunire, its earthly meaning known, and its heavenly connotation to be unveiled on that day. Examples abound: Aaron, Nadab, Abihu, Uzza, and Ahaziah.

Given the multitude of sore eyes and scarcity of surgeons, it's wise to withhold reproof until our own beams are cast out. This seems reasonable, for a person should heal themselves first. Nonetheless, many won't wait, leading Christ to appear indignant, labeling them hypocrites. Chrysostom asserts Christ's strong displeasure, as evidenced when He employs such words as "foolish servant," "painted tombs," "generation of vipers." Such language isn't used lightly.

The term "hypocrite" is reviled by both God and humans. As Octavius and Antonius hated a tyrant but not tyranny, we loathe a hypocrite but not hypocrisy. This aversion is visible in real hypocrisy; we cannot tolerate a fine list on coarse cloth, good appearance hiding inner decay, or a straight exterior disguising internal hollowness. In the state, poisoning or sword murder receives different punishments, the former being greater due to its hypocritical nature. Within the Church, fathers assigned severest penalties and penance for various sins, with hypocrisy bearing the heaviest punishment. Peter reacted sharply against Ananias and Sapphira; Paul listed false brethren among the gravest dangers. In Revelation, John prophesied that the Church would suffer greatly from those with women's faces and hair and lion's teeth. Prophets' complaints against them are marked by vivid imagery: pots with scum, cakes baked unevenly; ostriches with grand feathers but little flight. Christ specially condemns them, pronouncing seven woes, which He doesn't do for any other sinners. This sin is direly opposed to God.

To identify a hypocrite, we must evaluate their inner character. A father suggests we observe the exterior when admonishing; their outer aspect projects the removal of a mote, but their eye contradicts their tongue. The Syriac word means "face-taker"; their *mask* may be admonition, but it's fractured, revealing the true self beneath—an impudent hypocrite. Hypocrisy is a sign without substance, like donning a hood without learning underneath. Examples abound, more than we realize. We possess Elijah's mantle but not his spirit. Hypocrisy is a multidimensional sin, ranging from subtle to glaring. It affects us all. There are two kinds of it: one that talks and acts, and one that talks but doesn't act, manifesting as gross hypocrisy.

Hypocrisy has two objectives. God's glory should be sufficient motivation, yet we usually have another motive. The first and the best say more of themselves, but they do something; they commend more in word than in practice. The other are such as say and don't do anything, which is gross hypocrisy. Augustine says few aren't tainted by hypocrisy, though he amends that by asserting that surely not one is free from it. Actual hypocrisy has four types: delight in feigning goodness or intending evil, perilous hypocrisy concealed within a sheep's skin, hypocrites "uncased" or exposed, and hypocrites with visible "ears" hanging out—these are the broken-mask hypocrites. Playing the hypocrite doesn't require great intelligence; even an ass could be one, as anyone who can grasp them by the ears can call them hypocrites.

There are seven marks to identify a hypocrite in reproving someone. First, they observe things externally but not internally, as Master Beza noted. Hypocrites are superficial observers; they are referred to as spies, shifters, or sisters in Hebrew. A true Christian would rather see their own faults cast out (if they are weaknesses) and never acknowledge them. For instance, Shem and Japheth covered their father's nakedness without seeing it, while Ham saw and mocked it. These are the ones who proclaim others' imperfections. Joseph's example is different; he chose not to make Mary a public example despite his suspicions.

The second mark is that they never turn the spotlight on themselves; they lack the time and interest for introspection. When someone points out a flaw in their eye, they respond by critiquing the other person's eyes. Initially, they'll claim to have no issues at all, or partially deny it. If they admit it, they'll argue that it doesn't hinder their vision or that it could be better. Such hypocrites only expose minor faults, following the rhetorical principle that every sin can be mitigated.

The third mark is that they call others "brother." The Chaldean paraphrase advises us to observe the tongue, for it reveals the hypocrite. They greet their "brother" in the morning with a loud voice. Similarly, the Pharisees called Christ a good man without partiality, while privately considering him a Galilean.

The fourth mark is that they come with a sign, "let him alone;" they will only act as allowed, all in the name of love and charity. But if they have authority, they won't say, "Suffer me." As one says, "You don't negotiate with your beast." Similarly, in admonishing, you must do it, whether they agree or not.

The fifth mark is seen in hypocritical Ephraimites. The Tribe of Ephraim questioned why they weren't called. Good men, however, don't mind who performs a task, as long as it's done. Hypocrites reveal their desire for fame, not the act itself. They notice the glory of the act, not the act itself.

The sixth mark is their focus on *motes*. One might ask, "Don't these individuals have neighbors with beams in their eyes?" They certainly do. So why do they single out the brother with the mote? This is a sure sign of hypocrisy. As Chrysostom says, they do it to seem just or to halt criticism. They point out others' flaws to appear virtuous themselves. They aim to level the playing field by either rising higher or dragging others down, though they often can't accomplish the latter. Despite their tongues being their own, they feel confident to criticize those who are good.

The seventh mark is found in Matthew 23. They burden others but refuse to touch the burdens themselves, even with their smallest finger. They might say, "You're doing well to live so strictly," expecting others to be like angels while they act like devils. Other, more effective notes are listed in Matthew 23. Some might think that since hypocrisy is gross in reproving, they'll avoid it altogether. This mindset reveals fear or wicked subtlety, making these individuals worse than the former. Our disapproval of an hypocrite shouldn't exceed God's disapproval; His judgment should guide us. God condemns hypocrisy not for the exterior but for the interior. Reprehension is virtuous, but in hypocrites, it's tainted by other factors. Pharisees were reprovers, so our righteousness must surpass theirs. Augustine wisely advises that we can't cast off our skin because wolves sometimes wear it. Every external aspect in their hypocrisy is good, such as proselytizing and remembering saints. Hating them for their misuse would prove foolish in the end.

Another type may conclude that outward offenders aren't hypocrites, which is all they boast. Yet, by Christ's testimony, one with a beam in their eye is a *singular* hypocrite. Those who bear such marks are indeed *brethren* of hypocrites. Isaiah, speaking of wild youths, called them all *hypocrites*. Justin claims every evil person is a hypocrite, to some extent. They can even disguise themselves as angels of light, though their hearts remain in darkness.

The world is filled with hypocrites, exemplified by *tares*, often seen as bundles of hypocrites. Though not all are named as such, Matthew 23 includes Christ's statement: "Hypocrites, Isaiah prophesied well of you." Many bundles exist: those who only perform duties as far as men's precepts dictate. Some might marvel that Paul called some "the circumcision of God" and "the Israel of God," suggesting other Israels and circumcisions. Such as the circumcised of Parliaments and the Israelites of Princes, who would readily adopt Omri's statutes if Josiah's were abolished.

Another kind of hypocrite includes heretics like the Novatians, Anabaptists, and Familists. Worse are those within the Church who initially appear genuine until their mouths are filled. Some cloak their hypocrisy in feigned populism, like Absalom. They ally with great men to avoid trouble if they err. Others ally with good men; if that fails, they turn to statutes as in Daniel, or even to religion itself, as Pilate did with Christ.

Some think that assuming the duty of admonishing is itself hypocrisy. They believe they are not clean-handed but clean-hearted, glorious inside despite the world's view. However, James asserts they must be clean-handed as well. Augustine counters that one's pure conscience isn't sufficient; remember Christ's words too. Make your light shine before others so they see your good works and glorify your heavenly Father (Matthew 5). If there's a beam in your eye, there's a stack in your heart. Why then do they call those who are more careful hypocrites? Christ might call the Pharisees so, knowing their thoughts, but no prophet called someone a hypocrite without an internal beam. This is the devil's insidious tactic, vexing God's children with a sin that they can't easily disprove externally, making them *appear* even greater hypocrites. Gather all the saints and challenge them; see how they defend themselves. The truth is, two qualities are required of a Christian: God grants Job to be both straight outwardly and sound within.

A Treatise on Anger

"And it came to pass, as soon as he came nigh unto the camp, that he saw the calf, and the dancing: and Moses' anger waxed hot, and he cast the tables out of his hands, and brake them beneath the mount," (Exod. 32:19).

Moses, in the twelfth chapter of Numbers, is acclaimed as the meekest man on Earth. Yet, in Exodus 32:19, he's described as becoming angry, and this anger is both commended and permitted. From this, we learn that not all forms of anger are forbidden by the Word of God. Only the anger devoid of just cause, whether external or not, and the anger not aligned with the Word, are disallowed. Anger, like other mental attributes, can be evil when governed by our corruption, making it a work of the flesh, and thus proscribed by the Word. Yet, when sanctified and controlled by God's Spirit and Word, it becomes a commanded duty, a fruit of the Spirit. Numerous examples in Scripture show God's servants expressing anger for righteous causes, within bounds, and they are commended for it. We ought to follow their examples in similar situations.

To distinguish between spiritual and Christian anger and carnal anger, to discern the workings of God's Spirit versus corrupted fleshly actions, it's beneficial to outline differences using specific notes.

The first distinction lies in our response to offenses against us versus offenses against the Lord. If we can patiently endure and overcome personal insults and wrongs, yet exhibit fervent zeal and jealousy when it comes to the Lord's honor, it's indicative of righteous anger stemming from the Spirit of God. Conversely, when people react vehemently and swiftly to trifles, driven by their own interests, it originates from the flesh, and such anger is unacceptable. Spiritual anger isn't easily provoked; when it surfaces, it's proportionate to the offense: minor wrongs trigger brief, mild anger; greater wrongs result in more intense and extended anger. This echoes our Heavenly Father, who's *slow to wrath*, doesn't incessantly reprimand us, overlooks our errors, and doesn't repay us according to our deeds. He's more invested in cultivating our love for Him than instilling fear. We should emulate this approach, striving to be loved rather than feared, utilizing love to attract rather than fear to compel. This implies that before expressing anger, we should pray that the Lord guides us righteously, lest we stumble or sin.

Secondly, some people are perpetually discontented and become irate over trivial matters, a clear sign of evil anger emanating from the flesh. In contrast, spiritual anger is seldom stirred, and when it is, it's measured by the severity of the offense. A minor transgression evokes brief, mild anger; a major fault provokes more sustained and intense anger. We should resemble our Heavenly Father, who chides us sparingly, not continuously, and doesn't constantly scrutinize our misdeeds or retaliate *in kind*. He employs more means to inspire love for Him than fear. If someone realizes their hastiness in anger, they should recognize that such behavior promotes folly and that anger dwells within the realm of fools. Patient individuals manifest wisdom. They must understand that such anger is undesirable and should earnestly work to suppress it, employing prayer as a precursor to holy anger. If we fail to pray before anger emerges or when the opportunity arises, we ought to be wary of our anger's legitimacy, for we're at risk of stumbling and sinning.

Thirdly, it's a sign of Christian anger when we're indignant at sin regardless of the sinner's identity. Many individuals become incensed in personal matters, justifying their zeal for God's glory. However, if a sin doesn't directly involve them, they're apathetic. Such behavior unveils their lack of faith, love, and concern for God's glory. As God's honor is uplifted not only by our obedience but by others' as well, it's also diminished by others' sins. When a sin doesn't affect us, yet we're discontented and provoked, driven by genuine zeal for God's glory and love for our brethren, our anger is righteous.

Furthermore, some readily denounce offenses committed by enemies but tolerate the same actions from friends. In spiritual anger, the response is contrary; it's more forgiving toward enemies' faults than friends'. It more swiftly rebukes a friend's sin than an enemy's.

Therefore, friends who condone sin are *neither* desirable nor commendable. Open rebuke is superior to hidden affection; rebukes from a loved one are sweet. If a family member or close friend fell ill, we'd spare no effort to restore their health, else they might question our love. Similarly, in the spiritual illness of sin, neglecting efforts to rescue others from danger reveals a lack of love. When our friends sin, if our anger arises from zeal for God's cause and their salvation, if we blend love with anger to effectively reprove them, our anger is of the Spirit, not the flesh.

The fourth sign of Christian and spiritual anger, while bearing resemblance to the previous one, serves to differentiate them as much as any other distinction does. Many individuals are quick to condemn others' sins yet *fail* to be angry with their own. In response, the Lord admonishes them, saying: "Thou hypocrite, first cast out the beam out of thine own eye; and then shalt thou see clearly to cast out the mote out of thy brother's eye," (Matthew 7:5). Also, in another context, He declares: "He that is without sin among you, let him first cast a stone at her," (John 8:7). Therefore, if we can foremostly be angry with our own sins, more so than with others, even casting the first stone at ourselves, then our anger is of the Lord. No one can righteously be angry at the sins of others while failing to be grieved and angered by their own. When our anger begins with ourselves, for each sin within us, and we're unwilling to tolerate any sin within us or remain in it, and when no one is more troubled by our sins than ourselves, accusing and condemning ourselves more than anyone else can, and when we're apprehensive of sins not present in us and take measures against them, then if we're angry at others' sins, we can trust that our anger is good. Even if our anger is falsely accused of being tainted, whether in our own matters or against our adversaries, our consciences and hearts will testify otherwise, offering us solace.

Fifthly, there are those who, when they become angry with one person, are incensed with everyone, to the extent that anger consumes them, rendering them unfit for both Godly and brotherly duties. This anger is purely of the flesh and is to be condemned. If anger renders us unfit for hearing God's word or engaging in prayer, if it disturbs our minds and agitates us, even if it's in a noble cause and for God's sake, it's to be disapproved. The works of God's Spirit do not obstruct one another; they *mutually* enhance. If prayer was previously lukewarm, earnestness in God's cause ignites fervor for prayer. If attentiveness to the word was lacking, it's rekindled. Zeal and anger in the Lord's cause and for His glory inject vitality into every good endeavor. Genuine anger doesn't hinder our godly duties or reduce our love for our brethren; it rather stirs compassion toward them in light of the divine wrath hovering over them. Thus, we're spurred to pray more fervently for them, outweighing any impulse for retribution. Our concern shifts from punishing them to aiding them in overcoming sin. Therefore, in this anger for sin, loving compassion for the individual is intertwined, wherein anger isn't the driving force for revenge but rather pity for their condition. This highlights a pivotal distinction: Christian anger is coupled with sorrow for God's dishonor and our brother's harm, whereas carnal anger harbors joy and gratification, inflating the self. A prime example of righteous anger is seen in Christ's dealings with the Pharisees; He was both angry and sorrowful (Mark 3:5). Similarly, when He beheld Jerusalem's impending destruction due to their sins, anger culminated in *tears* (Luke 19:41). Similarly, when Paul threatens the Corinthians with discipline due to their sins, he admits that his impending visit might lead to his own sorrow, mourning the sinful actions of many (2 Corinthians 12:21). On the contrary, fleshly anger swells with pride when confronted with others' sins.

To cultivate holy anger for sin within us, we should strive to develop the same sentiment expressed by the Prophet David in Psalm 69:9, where he declares: "The reproaches of them that reproached thee are fallen upon me." David believed that each sin against God was also committed against himself. He was as troubled and angered by these sins as if they were his own. This was because the honor of God entrusted to his care had been tarnished, and God Himself dishonored. Such righteous anger and zeal should also dwell in us. To temper this ardor, avoiding excessive harshness, we must consider how the Apostle Paul interprets the same passage in Romans 15:3 when urging believers to bear with the weak. "For even Christ pleased not himself; but, as it is written, The reproaches of them that reproached thee fell on me," (Rom. 15:3). He cites the example of Christ, who suffered for the people's sins as if they were His own. Therefore, we should regard our brethren's sins as our own, inducing patience and compassion due to our shared humanity and the divine image our brethren bear. This mindset fosters a zealous anger merged with love and compassion for the individual.

Through these distinctive signs, genuine Christian and spiritual anger can be discerned from its carnal counterpart. By following the former, commanded by the law and instilled by God's Spirit, we can avoid the latter, forbidden by the law and stemming from our corrupted flesh. Neither should we be fools, continuously angry at every slight, nor should we embrace the heretical and blasphemous clan of fleshly love that rejects anger entirely. While other differences exist, a conscientious consideration and practice of these distinctions will simplify the recognition of the others.

FINIS

A Treatise on the Doctrine of Fasting

"Moreover when ye fast, be not, as the hypocrites, of a sad countenance: for they disfigure their faces, that they may appear unto men to fast. Verily I say unto you, They have their reward. But thou, when thou fastest, anoint thine head, and wash thy face; That thou appear not unto men to fast, but unto thy Father which is in secret: and thy Father, which seeth in secret, shall reward thee openly," (Matt. 6:16-18).

In Matthew 6, Jesus teaches that when fasting, one should prepare oneself secretly, not for the sake of impressing others, but for God, who sees in secret and rewards openly.

Isaiah 1:16 states that the fasting the Lord desires involves putting away evil thoughts, ceasing to do evil, learning to do good, seeking justice, helping the oppressed, assisting the fatherless, and addressing widows' complaints.

Isaiah 58 depicts fasting in a negative light when accompanied by a continuation of sinful behavior. It notes that fasting doesn't lead to righteous change, and even during fasting, people remain driven by their desires, engaged in violence, strife, and unrighteousness.

Zechariah 7:9 highlights that fasting without genuine acts of mercy is futile, emphasizing the importance of showing kindness and mercy to one's neighbors.

In Daniel 9, it's mentioned that Daniel prayed to the Lord with fasting.

Joel 2:12 encourages turning to the Lord through fasting, weeping, and mourning.

In 1 Samuel 7:6, the children of Israel fasted while confessing their sins to God.

Acts 14 records an instance where Paul and Barnabas prayed and fasted while ordaining Elders.

2 Corinthians 6:4 shows how Paul demonstrated his ministry of God through fasting and praying.

Luke 2:37 mentions Anna the Prophetess serving God through fasting and praying.

Various Psalms illustrate Jesus Christ's humbling of His soul, weakening of His knees, and becoming lean through fasting.

Different types of fasts exist, both general and private. Some, like the fast of Esther and Mordecai, are commanded generally but observed privately. Others, such as Ezra's fast on behalf of the Jews who had married foreign wives, are public and specific.

The concept of a general fast, observed in all places, cannot currently be fully realized due to the lack of fulfillment of necessary conditions. Circumstances like widespread wars, plagues, and famines might lead to general fasts as seen with the Ninevites. However, in the context of Scriptural commands, general fasts are meant to move us to mourn spiritual evils and prevent potential dangers. This understanding pertains to those truly instructed by God's Word to acknowledge their own sins and the sins of others, and to fear God's impending judgments.

Christ's teachings regarding patched clothing and new wine applies here, as true fasting might not be universally possible, but it's better to deliver the truth and set an example for emulation. Teaching and practicing true fasting helps dispel ignorance, prevent us from falling into carnal indulgence, refute erroneous opinions, and counter slanderous accusations regarding our perceived lack of fasting.

The necessity of fasting within our Church becomes evident due to our *abundance* of sins. Fasting should accompany prayer for the preservation of Religion and the State, as well as for the right division of the Word of God. This helps people recognize their sins, grasp the significance of changes in Religion and government, and comprehend both God's warnings and promises. Presently, our sins are more numerous, signs of God's wrath are more apparent, and concerns for danger in the Church and Commonwealth are greater. Hence, there's a need for extraordinary fasting to avert potential divine wrath.

One might question whether fasting weakens loyal subjects and emboldens enemies. This was unjustly hurled at Jeremiah by faithless, political rulers. Though some may argue that true faith weakens hearts and encourages enemies, such claims are baseless and not upheld by godly or wise men. Moreover, fasting doesn't uplift our enemies; rather, it exposes their pride and malicious intentions. Fasting doesn't embolden the Papists but exposes their wickedness.

The example of Israel's victories gained through faith, prayer, and fasting, as recorded in Scripture, supports the notion that victories require both faith and spiritual means. Although daily fasting is unnecessary, extraordinary fasting is crucial during times of urgency and danger. This exercise doesn't bolster enemies but rather confronts them with a God-fearing and repentant Church. Fasting should not be mistaken for continual sustenance, just as constant medical intervention isn't recommended. The same principle applies to spiritual nourishment and fasting. While we lament the lack of diligent preaching, we should not *mistakenly* consider sporadic preaching sufficient.

Scripture emphasizes that ministers should always keep knowledge, crying out ceaselessly, for God's hand is stretched out all day. The ministry of the Word of God is as vital as nourishment for both the spiritually young and mature. While some argue that fasting weakens, history and experience attest that true fasting strengthens the faithful. While outward means of defense are necessary, they're most effective when used alongside spiritual means. Fasting is not meant to replace spiritual reliance but to humble ourselves and emphasize God's power and goodness.

As we face our sins and impending dangers, we should acknowledge our shortcomings through fasting, repentance, and faith. Fasting is not a constant exercise but a *deliberate* response to *specific* needs. Fasting every day is excessive and unscriptural, leading to unproductiveness and physical ailments. Instead, temperate and moderate use of God's provisions (sobriety) should be our norm, distinct from complete abstinence (fasting). Extremes must be avoided; Martin Bucer's teaching on this suggests either abstaining from fasting entirely or fasting in moderation.

Simply abstaining from daily meals while indulging in life's pleasures and luxuries is not a true fast. It's important to differentiate between temperate living and complete abstinence. Even the austere diet of John the Baptist, while appropriate for his circumstances, should not be universally imposed (locusts and wild honey). The need for fasting isn't daily or constant, but rather prompted by specific occasions.

The hyperbolic expressions of prayer and fasting, along with the continuous presence in the Temple by the aged widow Anna, do not establish that a daily fasting regimen should be practiced by those who lead active lives, whether in civil or ecclesiastical spheres. Those engaged in active and busy lives can bear the mental and physical strains due to their age and vocation. They are obligated by their calling to devote six days of the week to work and the seventh to celebrate the Lord, not to engage in a Manichean-style daily fast.

Examples of David, Daniel, and Paul are celebrated for their devout practices of prayer and fasting. David maintained a daily practice according to his regular needs, while Daniel and Paul resorted to fasting on special and extraordinary occasions, prompted by God's leading. However, following Christ's example, daily fasting is far from accurate, as His life was considered a continuous feast despite certain instances of fasting. While the Popish daily fast might have physical implications, it poses spiritual dangers and is to be rejected.

A true fast doesn't merely entail bodily emptiness, for the kingdom of heaven isn't determined by food and drink. Eating doesn't worsen us, nor does abstaining improve us significantly. Physical exercise brings little profit and can often harm the mind by inflating it rather than humbling it. Instead, spiritual exercises such as prayer, reading, and meditation should be pursued alongside fasting. These means nourish the inward man as we suppress the outward, humbling both aspects. We await God's timing for spiritual sustenance just as we anticipate physical nourishment.

In addition, a genuine fast involves abstaining from routine indulgences and finding solace in multiple sermons, fervent prayer, divine meditation, Scripture reading, and psalm singing. The Prophets Isaiah and Joel emphasized not only personal repentance but also communal fasting. Nehemiah, Ezra, and the people exemplified this practice, utilizing fasting as a means of seeking God's mercy beyond regular Word-based worship.

If we were as discerning and conscientious as our predecessors, we would recognize more significant divine judgments and deeper spiritual maladies within ourselves. Our times are marred by an *ignorant* and *dissolute* ministry, improper impropriations, irreligious patrons, lax Protestant living, unyielding Papists, deceitful atheists and Machiavellians within the Church and society, ongoing disputes among genuine believers, and more. Amidst this, we neglect the suffering of our persecuted brethren. Isn't the Lord sounding the trumpet for our fasting? Let the ministers of the Lord continually exhort us to heed this call. May they rebuke sin, proclaim the law, inspire repentance, and promote fasting.

FINIS

Notes on Our Salvation

Here are true indicators of our salvation:
1. We recognize the importance of searching the Scriptures to find Christ and eternal life, just as people seek silver and gold (Proverb 2:4).
2. We value the word of God more than our daily sustenance and desire to be spiritually nourished and grow through it (Job 23:12; 1 Peter 2:1-3).
3. We exhibit swiftness to hear, slowness to speak, and restraint from anger, setting aside malice and sin's negative aspects. We receive the implanted word with meekness, allowing it to save our souls, and obey the doctrine delivered to us (James 1:21; Romans 6:17).
4. We engage in meditating on the Word day and night, desiring that all our actions, words, and thoughts *align* with it (Joshua 1; Psalm 1, 119).
5. We long for *holy* assemblies and find delight in observing the Sabbath (Psalm 84; Psalm 122:1; Isaiah 58).
6. We hold ministers in high regard, joyfully ministering to them with our goods (Acts 10:16; Romans 10:15; Galatians 6).

The necessity of an upright heart is proven by its consequences:

1. Without it, we can't be certain of justification and sanctification in Christ Jesus (Psalm 32:2; Hebrews 10:22).
2. Without it, we can't be sure of genuine repentance from our sins (Joel 2:12; Ezekiel 18:22-23).
3. Without it, we can't be confident that our ways please God (Psalm 119:1, 5, 10-11, 80).
4. Without it, God's word won't bear fruit in our lives (Luke 8:12, 16).
5. Without it, our prayers won't be acceptable to God (1 Timothy 2:8; Psalm 119:58, 145; Psalm 66:18).
6. Without it, we can't be sure of our true baptism (1 Peter 3:21; Matthew 3:8; Romans 2:29).
7. Without it, we can't receive the Sacrament of the Lord's Supper to our comfort (2 Chronicles 30:18-19; Psalm 45).
8. Without it, fasting lacks its intended significance (Daniel 10:12).
9. Without it, genuine worship of God is unattainable (1 John 4:24; Isaiah 29:13; Psalm 15:2; Psalm 24:4).
10. Without it, we'll never see God (Matthew 5:8; Psalm 15:2; Psalm 24:4).
11. Without it, we won't receive blessings from God but may experience confusion and destruction (Psalm 125:4-5; Psalm 119:6; Psalm 7:10; Psalm 80).

Marks of a true and upright heart include:
1. Belief that God the Father, through Jesus Christ's blood and the Holy Spirit's work, cleanses us from our sins.
2. Belief that the Spirit proceeding from the Father and the Son cleanses us through the Word. We obey the Word's commands, regardless of human advice or commands.
3. A genuine desire to avoid outward situations that might lead to sin or relapse.
4. Mourning over initial inclinations to sin and fear of future yielding.
5. Eagerness to use all means prescribed in God's Word to attain purity of heart.
6. *Consistent* adherence to these principles, whether privately or publicly.
7. Seeking God's approval without seeking praise or profit from others, primarily seeking His kingdom and righteousness (Matthew 6).

FINIS

The Sending of the Holy Spirit

Acts 2:14-17, "But Peter, standing up with the eleven, lifted up his voice, and said unto them, Ye men of Judaea, and all ye that dwell at Jerusalem, be this known unto you, and hearken to my words: For these are not drunken, as ye suppose, seeing it is but the third hour of the day. But this is that which was spoken by the prophet Joel; And it shall come to pass in the last days, saith God, I will pour out of my Spirit upon all flesh: and your sons and your daughters shall prophesy, and your young men shall see visions, and your old men shall dream dreams."

In the earlier part of this chapter, the work of God is described in sending down the Holy Spirit on the Apostles, and also the effects of this, both in the Apostles and in the listeners; wonderful in one way and diverse in the other. The Apostles spoke with strange tongues. The listeners were not greatly moved, but they secretly murmured and said, they had drunk deeply and thus became eloquent. Whereupon Peter, seizing this good opportunity, refuted them by two reasons: first, telling them it was only nine o'clock, or the third hour of the day, a time when men do not usually get drunk. "No," says he, "we are not drunk, as you suppose; the opposite is true with us. For what has happened is not an excess of drink, but an abundance of God's spirit, promised not just to us alone but to all genders, conditions, and states of people, if you are ready to receive it. For just as the Lord has bestowed the gifts of His spirit on us, so He will also do it for you, if you do not *willfully* refuse. Therefore, the Lord is ready to work wonders in the world; and whoever knowingly refuses or carelessly misuses these graces will be caught in these judgments. Yet the Lord, being more ready to magnify His mercy than to show His justice, will fulfill this, that whoever calls on the name of the Lord will both escape the judgments threatened and also obtain these." And this briefly and generally sums up the meaning of this passage.

More specifically, we can observe three special points: first, the liberal testimony of Joel, and his rich praise of God's grace in bestowing such gifts on His Church under the kingdom of Jesus Christ, set down in verses 17 and 18. The second thing is that when the Lord will deal with His people this way, He will send many judgments, such as heresies, offenses, famines, plagues, and wars. These are described in symbolic and metaphorical terms like blood, fire, vapor of smoke, and the like, through which He will punish and avenge Himself for the contempt of such gracious mercies, as in verses 19 and 20. The third thing is the means by which we will escape these heavy judgments and attain these heavenly graces, and then persevere in them, which is declared in verse 21.

Before we consider further into the depth of this discourse and these particular points, we will observe the context and the details of Peter's speech: the occasion was that the people, not benefiting from the prior marvelous work of the Lord, prompted the Apostle to further instruct those willing to learn and to reprove the scoffers. Yet he was not so offended at them, for not being benefited by God's wonderful works, that he ceased all instruction; instead, he stirred himself more earnestly and endeavored to teach them familiarly.

From this, we must learn not to be rashly, suddenly, or thoughtlessly too offended at the lack of progress, little progress, or backsliding of some; but rather we must labor to approach the matter anew, always remembering that not only a woe is threatened to those who cause genuine offense but also to those who take offense in Christ. Therefore, looking at ourselves in natural or spiritual gifts, we must test ourselves, how patiently we can endure without offense either the lack of or resistance to similar gifts in others. Yet we see that if, after some effort, people progress slowly and do not make such rapid progress as is desired, most are ready to abandon all and are glad to escape the duty they owe, thinking themselves exempted and as if discharged. When spiritual people in such cases think themselves to be spurred to greater earnestness and more painstaking use of means; to such well-meaning minds and people of upright hearts, the Lord often grants increased gifts so that they may employ them for the benefit of others.

Certainly, if flesh and blood could judge in such a case, we might think that this present occasion could have caused Peter to abandon the people; but he, more gently and modestly, as the leader of the inquiry, continued the matter and answered them as we have heard. We may read in Acts 6 how a murmur arose between the Jews and the Greeks, to the point where the Apostles' credibility began to be questioned. They were accused of neglecting the widows, a duty belonging to them, as if they held faith in God with respect to persons. This might seem able to discourage them, but on the contrary, through the blessing of God's Spirit, they recognized their own shortcomings and began to seek new ministries. If they had taken the matter too much to heart, they might have become unprofitable, but meekly overlooking the offense and wisely attending to God's counsel, they recognized themselves as mere men, who could not be infinitely occupied or busy in many things, and so ordained Deacons in the Church.

We must make particular use of this when, for some good means used, or otherwise when much unkindness is shown to us, even by our friends, or when we find little thanks for our labor or sometimes reap reproaches from their hands as our reward; then we must not grow lax in our duties or grow cold in love and falter in our affection towards them. If we do, we will reveal that our affection was merely and only natural, not spiritual. It is true, and cannot be denied, that a kind heart and generous spirit are most hurt by reproaches, but this offense must be overcome, and fought against in us, following the example of both Peter in our present text and the rest of the Apostles in that earlier place, Acts 6. They took the occasion to accuse themselves rather than cease to be profitable to the Church of Christ. It is not, nor should it seem to us, a strange thing that God's graces and gifts have found such a cold reception, or even, more contrary, great opposition. We see that although the Apostles were greatly filled with God's Spirit and performed miracles, yet they were accused of drunkenness.

Therefore, we must not be offended, when we consider that our own condition is far below theirs; if the same contempt happens to us, we must endure it patiently and continue our service to God and His Church, and not withdraw our hands or slacken our affections, as is the usual manner of weak minds. Again, we see that Peter was not content with these effects alone, but that God's work must be further opened and declared by His word. Therefore, let us not think that our labor will be in vain, nor that we will be able to perform much or anything at all *without the ministry of the word*. This is the instrument God uses to teach and convert men, to gather and build them up in His Church, and this is the way He reveals Himself to His own, by His word and sacraments, and therefore no other way must be devised or practiced by us.

Certainly, it will be seen in the end that this ministry alone shall be approved, and it shall stand forever, and whatever else is practiced and esteemed among men, if it is not found to be grounded upon this foundation, it shall fall and come to nothing, as we see many errors and false doctrines have done in these last and dangerous times. We see, therefore, that Peter did not despise the use of the word; but rather seeing God's work, he esteemed it more highly, knowing that the Word must be joined with it. Therefore, let us not be content with feeling some motions of God's spirit within us, but let us go further and search the Scriptures, praying to God that He would open our eyes to see and our ears to hear, and our hearts to understand the wonderful things contained in His law. He has not promised to work without means, or to teach us without His word, and therefore we must not forsake it but constantly attend upon it.

Certainly, we must make the word of God our rule, our square, our balance, and our touchstone, to try and examine both ourselves and others, our thoughts and affections, our judgments and decisions, whether they agree with God's word, and if we find them contrary, we must condemn them. For surely the Spirit of God will never lead us into any other way than what is revealed to us in the word, and if we wander from it, we can be sure that we are not led by the Spirit of God but by our own spirit. To confirm this, we must remember what the Apostle says in Gal. 1:8, "Though we or an angel from heaven preach any other gospel unto you than that which we have preached unto you, let him be accursed."

Therefore, this ministry of the word must be attended to diligently, and we must make this our chief study, to know and understand God's will revealed in His word. This must be our daily labor and earnest endeavor; then we may hope to be both taught and led by His Holy Spirit into all truth, and so escape the dangerous rocks and fatal precipices, against which many have struck and made shipwreck of their faith. Thus, we may avoid those deceivers, who by the sleight of their hands and cunning craftiness, lay in wait to deceive. By this way, we may walk safely in the midst of so many snares, being led and guided by God's Spirit through His word, to the glory of His name and our everlasting salvation, to which may God bring us all, through our Lord and Savior Jesus Christ.

In the last days, meaning when Christ should be revealed in the flesh, preached to the Gentiles, believed on in the world, and taken up in glory, these gifts of the Spirit will be abundant. This time is called *the last day* because of the stability of the Church and the perfection of the word, as we look for no other doctrine until Christ comes in judgment. "Now all these things came unto them for examples, and they are written for our admonition, upon whom the ends of the world are come," (1 Corinthians 10:11). After the Apostle had instilled fear in the Corinthians with the example of the Jews, he comes to apply his doctrine in this way. It is as if he was saying, these things were not meant to serve them alone, but also us in the last days. And in Hebrews 1, it is clearly and evidently phrased, "At sundry times and in divers manners God spoke in times past to our fathers by the Prophets; in these last days, He has spoken to us by His Son," *etc.* All these places, in meaning at least, agree with this place, along with Galatians 4:4, where it is referred to *as the fullness of time.*

Before Christ's coming, the state of the people was childish and pedagogical, and therefore people, like John's disciples, looked for another who should come. The Samaritans had a general principle among them that the Messiah, when he came, would restore all things and put them in order. From this, we must learn not to look for any new doctrine or revelations from men. Christ Himself has come and has made things perfect; Christ, the prince of Prophets whom they were looking for, is manifest in the flesh. The closer the Prophets were to Him, the clearer was their sight of Him; the farther they were from Him, the dimmer was their knowledge of Him.

The Lord Himself has spoken, and the book is now closed with a complete conclusion. If anyone takes away from the words of it, God shall take away his part from the book of life; if anyone adds to it, God shall add to him the plagues threatened in the book. Therefore, all Heretics, Papists, and Turks will not hesitate to agree in this common error. The Turk, though he does not deny Christ and the scripture, and gives them their time and place, will make a way for his Mahomet, who must interpret the word to him as he pleases. The Papist does not plainly deny Christ and His Gospel but does not see all sufficiency in it. Complaining of some defect, he looks to unwritten verities and leans on old traditions to be given to the Church, and therefore he will have the Pope to be Christ's vicar, and whatever their Synods conclude must be established as Catholic truth, measuring the scriptures by their traditions and not their traditions by the scriptures.

The damnable *Family of Love* treats the word (which is fearful even to think of, much less to speak of) like a nose of wax or a shipman's hose, yet they will have their main teacher Mr. H.N., who is the eighth person and the last man, who must be joined with the Gospel. They will agree as far as he and other gray-headed, illuminated elders interpret the Scriptures. We, against these and all other *heretics* confessing the scriptures of God to be perfect and absolute for salvation, join no other thing with them, but say that we live in the last days when Christ left the fullness of doctrine, prayer, sacraments, and discipline to the Church by His Apostles. Therefore, we don't mind revelation, Mahometical interpretation, nor traditions of men, but even if an Angel comes from heaven with an unwritten verity varying from God's word, we utterly reject him.

Neither do we completely and simply refuse all Church orders, even if sometimes there is no express word. If by consequence, cause, or effect we find it agreeable or not repugnant to the word, after trial with the holy scriptures, we will accept it. The heretics will not agree to make the word the touchstone. Moreover, as in all other arts, those who wish to attain sound knowledge must credit the principles; otherwise, as even the heathens saw, there is no further dealing in learning them. We have specific general truths and rudiments by which we bring newcomers to Christ and test both old and young by them, which our heretics won't admit.

    We hold certain general rules about God's power, providence, and wisdom, our redemption and salvation by Jesus Christ, our effective sanctification, the forgiveness of our sins, the hope of glorious resurrection, and a better life, obedience, prayer, discipline, and holy conversation in spite of all heretics. Against these, even though they argue, declaim, rail, and write, we will never lose our grip. Secondly, a thing unfamiliar to these men, we make it a point to mark the writer's scope and purpose. We compare what goes before with what comes after, we compare one place with another, the Old Testament with the New, the allegories with the plain speeches. We see a perfect harmony in the scriptures, and we reject all dissenting and disagreeing doctrines from the scriptures. Neither the Turk, Papist, nor Familist will do this, so we have the truth in these last days, which neither Mahomet, the Bishop of Rome, nor Mr. H.N. have. We will not be judged by their revelations, traditions, and dreams but by the scriptures, by which we judge them. We say the last days or fullness of time because we have the truth.

However, the vilest wretches who fill up the measure of their sins will not hesitate to say with us that these are the last days, interpreting it to mean whoever enters the house of love and is enlightened is now risen again, has heard the last trumpet, and has become of an angelic nature, needing no eating, drinking, or marrying, like men. These are our wandering rogues who will tie themselves to no calling but live as they think in the resurrection. It's clear how necessary it is to understand this phrase correctly about the last days. We don't call them the last days because no further time shall be, but because these days shall not end until Christ comes and gives up the kingdom to God the Father. These last days began at His first coming in humility in the flesh and will end at His last coming in glory to judgment.

It follows in our text, "In the last days," says God. All the Scriptures are worthy to be heard because they come from God, not from man, although man may be the instrument of the Holy Ghost. Therefore, it is said, "First know this, that no prophecy in Scripture is of private origin. For the prophecy did not come in old times by the will of man, but holy men of God spoke as they were moved by the Holy Ghost," (2 Peter 1:20-21). The Prophets, to wholly disavow themselves in all their significant messages, used to say: "Thus says the Lord of hosts; Thus says the Lord, the Holy One," and similar phrases. By this, they sought to gain greater credibility, diverting people's thoughts from any notion of human doing, and directing their faith to acknowledge that it comes from God. Therefore, we must listen to the word as though we were hearing God Himself speaking to us, yes, as though we either went up to heaven, or God came down to us. Likewise, whether we read, hear, or meditate privately, we must always consider ourselves in the presence of God, who closely observes the pure use of His holy word, remembering that holy speech of Cornelius, "Now we are all here present before God, to hear all things commanded thee by God," (Acts 10:33). It is also said in the exhortation to praise God, "Let us come before his face with praise, *etc.*" (Psalm 95:2). This awareness will humble us when we realize that we are in the presence of God and His Angels, whose presence is described in Ezekiel 1. Therefore, the Apostle in 1 Corinthians 11:10, to persuade the women of Corinth even more, tells them that they are in the presence of the Angels. This consideration fosters *reverence* in hearing, without which we remain unmoved by a man's speaking, no matter how much he threatens, promises, menaces, comforts, exhorts, or reproves. No, we cannot be truly affected until we can say, *Surely it is the Lord who speaks to us; it is the word of the Most High God uttered by man; we will not accept it as the doctrine of men but of God, either as the teaching to save our souls or to condemn us; it's the mighty power of salvation if we believe, or a mighty power to cast us down to hell if we do not believe. It's the word of God that moves us, not the word of man.* For how could a Turk influence a Papist, or a

Papist move a Turk? If he takes away Muhammad's dreams from the Turk, or the Father's traditions from the Papist, or the eighth man's revelations from the Familist, and confronts them with the word, they are gone; so it is only the word of God, despite the devil, that dispels all their errors and is able to move them and convert as many of them to the truth as God wills to save. Thus, we see what the persuasion of God's presence and the authority of His word work within us. Now, before we proceed to other particulars, let us briefly consider the reasoning used here.

Earlier, he employed a reason of likelihood from the circumstance of time; now he turns to a reason of necessity because never could drunken men speak the wonderful things of the Spirit. This argument is drawn from opposites: men full of drink cannot thus reveal the works of God; men endowed with God's spirit cannot be drunken. In this manner, Paul reasons, "Be not drunk with wine, wherein is excess, but be filled with the Spirit," (Ephesians 5:18). As if he were saying: if you are filled with wine, there is excess; if you strive for excess of wine, you surely cannot have the Spirit. Christ also uses this argument: "No man can serve two masters, *etc.*" If a man wholly dedicates himself to God, he cannot serve the world; if all our mind, heart, and affections are given to the world, we cannot serve God. Those who are filled with wine and are drunken cannot have the Holy Ghost. I say drunken because otherwise, there would be no reason. For one may drink wine moderately and yet speak wonderfully of the works of God, and a man may, after eating and drinking, express the graces and praises of God to show that he has not immoderately abused God's creatures. It is a clear argument by which we may prove to ourselves that if, after our meal, we can discreetly, reverently, and humbly speak of things to God's praise and glory, we have not been immoderate or intemperate devourers of His gifts. This is a valuable argument and worthy of our reflection. In whatever worldly thing we exceed, we cannot apply ourselves to God's kingdom. For if the kingdom of God is our greatest delight, we shall use this world as though we used it not. We often marvel that after the word preached, our prayers made, the *sacraments* received, there still appears no change or alteration in us; our affections are as they were, our life is the same as it was before. But we do not consider that before we came to the word, prayer, and sacraments, our hearts were loaded and balanced with worldly cares, leaving no room in our affections for the word, and that our hearts were so crowded and thronged with vain pleasures that there was no room for God's Spirit to reside in us, and for religion to dwell among us. The proper consideration of this must wean us from the world and gluttonous pleasures, which lock up our hearts so that the Lord cannot enter in. We cannot simultaneously run with the hare and hold with the hound; we cannot hold fire and water together; we cannot reconcile Christ and Belial, light and darkness, God and the devil. If one is up, the other must be down; if one is down, the other will rise. Again, we marvel that after the word preached, we are so overtaken with our habitual pleasures and profits, seeing that while we did hear, we had a secret and sweet disliking of sin, and a self-reproach for the same, as long as these afterthoughts correct the former. Surely, I answer from Paul, "because we are yet carnal, we are more carnal than spiritual, we are babes in Christ, we have but young beginnings in Christ but old proceedings in the world," (2 Corinthians 3:3). Why then do we come to God so hesitatingly and limping? It's because we have not come to any good growth in new birth. However, let us beware that we do not continue to be weaklings, lest it results in *sickness unto death* of both body and soul. If we were more spiritual than carnal, had the Spirit poured upon us in some abundant measure, and were fully persuaded of God's providence watching over us, the ministry of His holy Angels waiting on us, and assured of the glory of the life to come, feeling the mighty power of the word, the law to humble us, the Gospel to foster faith in us, the sacraments to seal us, and Christ to live in us, this assurance would quickly cast off all our carnal affections. It would then rise to things above with an admiration and longing for Christ, and unite us to the Lord, so that as His nature is immaterial and spiritual, it would convert us into the same nature, and we would, "love the things above, not things on the earth," and we would feel the efficacy of this divine word more lively, to our everlasting comfort.

In the last days, I will pour out my Spirit upon all flesh, etc. This has now come to pass, and therefore Christ's kingdom is now here. Because whenever God's Spirit shall come upon all, then the kingdom of Christ is come, but now God's Spirit has come upon all, therefore the kingdom of Christ is now here. This is how the Apostle teaches us how we may know when and where Christ's kingdom is, even where both the young and the old, the women and the men, the servants and the masters can show forth the works of the Lord. In Popery, men and women, old and young, masters and servants, could not talk about the mysteries of God, therefore in Popery, Christ's kingdom is not there. And although our compound Anabaptists have great things in their mouths, yet because their men and women speak nothing but dreams, forsaking the word of God, they do not have the kingdom of Christ. In many places in the days of Queen Mary, both old and young were not afraid to show the praise of God, as well women, as men boldly professed the truth; not only masters but servants gave testimony to the Gospel with their blood, and therefore then in such places this kingdom appeared. And we may safely reason this way in every congregation at this day, where old and young, men and women, can speak the praise of God, there is the Spirit of God, there is the kingdom of Christ; otherwise, if these things are not there, there is not His kingdom, whatever means are used.

And now to branch out these words more particularly, first we are to note that God bestows such an excellent thing as His Spirit; secondly, that so excellent a thing is sent to so vile a thing as flesh; thirdly, this grace is not leased out to a few here and there, but is freely offered to all sorts, ages, sexes, and conditions of men; fourthly, it is not distilled by thin drops, but poured out in full measure and plentiful abundance. What is more vile than flesh? What is more precious than the Spirit of God? The excellence of which we shall see more evidently, Joel 2, where after the Prophet had severely threatened the Jews and exhorted them to convert, he comforts them again by promising unto them the renewing of God's mercies, and not only telling them how the Lord would again send them corn, wine, and oil, but at last reminds them of that which counterbalances all the rest, and says that the Lord will give them His Spirit to be poured out upon all flesh, which may seal and season all His other benefits, and which should never leave them until they had come to life everlasting. Above all gifts in the world, this is the gift of gifts, the Spirit of God, in which the Lord prefers us not only above all other earthly creatures but also above many men like ourselves, while He makes us Kings, Priests, and Prophets by pouring the same spirit upon us. The excellence of this benefit Christ Himself teaches us, where He teaches the people to pray, saying, "Which of you, if your child shall ask you for a piece of bread, will instead of bread give him a stone, etc.? If you, who are evil, know how to give good things to your children when they ask them, how much more shall your heavenly Father give you good things," says Matthew, "His Spirit," says Luke (Matthew 7:9-11, Luke 11:11-13)? This is the top, this is the head, this is the height, this is the depth of all good things, even the Spirit. Now, if this is eternal life, John 17:3, to know the Father to be the only true God, and whom He has sent, Jesus Christ, and no man can ever do this but by the spirit of God, by which we know and believe this according to the word, and so live forever; who will deny this gift of all gifts to be most principal? If this is the dignity of dignities, that we are the children of God and heirs of a better life, how precious a thing is it to have the privilege of God's own Spirit, which gives us the full title, interest, and assurance of all these things to us?

Again, if this is the fullness of our rejoicing in the day of Christ, that He is made of God unto us wisdom, and righteousness, and sanctification, and redemption, and that through Him we are as fully and more assuredly perfect, as ever Adam was in his creation, and we cannot have this wisdom, unless the Spirit tells us, how we are cleared thereby from our ignorance, we cannot rejoice in this righteousness, unless the spirit assures us, that by it we are acquitted from our guiltiness; we can have no comfort in that holiness until we know by God's Spirit, it answers for our impurity and profaneness, and so separates us and puts us apart to the works of sanctification, we cannot triumph in our redemption

The Sending of the Holy Spirit

until the comforting Spirit of God stays our impatient spirits by an undoubted expectation for the glorious appearing thereof; without this Spirit all things are death, but with this all things are *life*. This brings knowledge in the things of which we are ignorant; this brings to our remembrance the things which we have known and forgotten; this assures us of things in which we have been wavering; this joins us to God and unites us to Christ; when we go astray, we come home by the Spirit; when by it we are renewed, and by the same, we are established, come life, come death, come honor, come dishonor, prosperity, adversity, wealth or woe, the one shall not lift us up too much, the other shall not cast us down too much. If the Lord gives us a healthy body, credit, riches, and authority, we are hereby resolved to glorify God by these things, to redeem the time, and to possess them as though we possessed them not: if the Lord denies us these things, and sends sickness, discredit, poverty, and obscurity, the Lord will send a recompense of inward things, and wanting bodily health, He will give the salvation of our souls; instead of outward credit, we shall have credit with God, and be well thought of among His children; and if wanting worldly riches, we are enriched with heavenly things, we have lost nothing, having changed dross and dung for gold.

Without this, *wit* becomes subtlety, wisdom worldly policy, authority is armed to tyranny, dignity breeds ambition, riches engender covetousness.

Medicine becomes unfaithfulness, Law proves craftiness, Divinity degenerates into heresy; to be brief, all good things abused, turn to bad things. With this Spirit, weak things become strong, low things become excellent, vile things become precious, bitter things become sweet, common things become holy, and earthly things become heavenly. Even with the Spirit, our lives are full of dead works, and therefore we are to clear ourselves of these dead works, that we may serve the living God; but without the Spirit, all is dead. Without the Spirit of God, we cannot so much as *ask* for the Spirit of God.

Therefore, let us humbly entreat the Lord to pour His Spirit upon us more and more every day, that we may have a good understanding in all things, and so think and speak of God and His ways, as He has declared Himself in His word, so let us believe, speak, and live, and that we may never forget that the end of our faith is the salvation of our souls, and the end of our life is the beginning of our eternal happiness, where we shall know God as He is, and enjoy Him forever. Let us always remember that if we have not His Spirit, we are not His, that the Spirit is the earnest and seal of our salvation; if we have not the Spirit, we have no faith, no assurance of a better life; if we *have not the Spirit*, we have no love to God, no love to His children, no delight in His ways; and therefore, if we want the Spirit, we want all; if we have the Spirit, we have all. For He is given to us for a comforter, a guide, a counselor, a helper, a quickener, an illuminator, to lead us, to teach us, to strengthen us, to comfort us in all our ways, and therefore, let us entreat the Lord to pour Him upon us, that we may have Him in our hearts, in our mouths, in our lives, and that we may see and say, the Lord is our portion, and we shall not be moved.

On the contrary, if along with these good gifts we possess the Spirit of God, what significant good might we do in the Church or the Commonwealth? If in addition to the beauty of God's Spirit, we have the flowers of external things, what a unique ornament is this to our garland? What more can I say? In affliction, the Spirit shows us the hand of God both in humbling and comforting us, revealing our sins, cultivating in us the contempt for this life, the longing for the life to come, and thus sanctifying our cross by wisdom, repentance, and patience. Since these are the effects of God's Spirit, and it grants us through faith everlasting inheritance, assures us of all our rich treasures in Jesus Christ, seeing that it sanctifies all inner gifts and seasons the use of all external things; briefly, seeing that with it all things that seem miserable are most blessed, and without it, all things that seem happy are most miserable, it follows that of all gifts, the Holy Spirit is the most excellent. However, there is one thing to be added here, so that we may entirely separate ourselves from the Anabaptists; we speak of the Spirit, as it shows its power in us and works in us through the ministry of the Word, which two work together, and therefore it is said, "My words are spirit and life," (John 6:63). For without the Spirit, the Word is like the bright sun to a blind man, who, not because of the fault of a pure object, but for lack of sense, cannot discern the clearest thing in the world: and therefore, the Prophet David in Psalm 119 says, "Open my eyes, O Lord, that I may see the wonders of your law." Indeed, the sun is bright, but what is that to a blind man? The Word is glorious, but what is that to a man without the Spirit of God? For we profit by the Word as much as we receive its power through the inner ministry of the Spirit; we must test the spirits by the Word, and we will then know that we have received the Spirit of God when it gives us pure understanding, careful reception, and zealous practice of the same. Carnal men and our recent Anabaptists are merely boasters of themselves, claiming to be spiritual men: we are not taught to boast of the Spirit, or any of its works, except as it is guaranteed to us by the written Word. We admit that our mind is blind, and that we cannot profit from the Word except through God's Spirit. We do not look for the Spirit in our imagination, but for the Spirit that works through the Word; the same Spirit that spoke through Abraham, the Patriarchs, Moses, the Prophets, Paul and the Apostles, and through our Savior Christ himself. Seeing that the Spirit of God is such a high thing, we are here to complain about why we chase after life, profit, and pleasure, and have so little care to obtain God's good Spirit, which is so precious. It is a great fault to fancy so much the things of this world and so little to value this.

And here, not as part of a set treatise but by the way, we will speak of the last part of our division, that is, the means of *how to attain* these graces of the Spirit. We know rich men can attend fairs for their increase, ambitious men can gain advancement, carnal men will watch for their opportunities, and everyone in their kind knows how to best provide for their profit and pleasure. Our way is the opposite, and lies in careful listening to the Word, fervent use of prayer, respectful and fruitful attending of the Sacraments, and the most holy submission to the discipline of the Lord, frequenting the company of God's children, and weaning ourselves from the world; by all these means the Spirit may have a more voluntary, free, and complete work in and upon us. And although all these things are not specifically listed here, yet notice that here is named the most proper means pointing at all the rest, and this, as you see, is prayer, by which the Lord conveys his Spirit into us, making all other means more pleasant and profitable to us. Why then are not so many sermons nowadays more effective when one or two sermons touched these people so powerfully? Certainly, God's Spirit does not work in us as it did in them. Why, when anyone is converted, do so few turn to the Lord, when the Lord drew so many of these men at once to Himself? It's because we are drawn away too much by our own flesh and do not taste the sweetness of God's Spirit as they did. But can a man pray for faith and God's Spirit, which he neither has faith nor the Spirit of God as yet? Whatever good gift we have, it is certain that we have it by faith and God's Spirit in some measure in us, and then we can pray for an increase of them in us. For it is God's Spirit that prays in us, "Likewise the Spirit also helpeth our infirmities," (Romans 8:26). Indeed, many have received God's Spirit before they feel it, and faith before they see it, and by these means, they pray to receive faith and the Spirit of God, which is therefore said to be the gift of God. In this, they have found that God has granted them before they asked, and by this means, we must receive the same. If we feel an absence of the Spirit and faith, it is because of our lack of these means, or the lack of true use of these means, or lack of fervent prayer to the Lord, or lack of true faith in the name of the Lord Jesus Christ.

Then remember for your comfort the covenant God made with us, that is, God will pour out His Spirit on all flesh, and you will receive His power if you complain truthfully and not like a parrot imitating the work of reason. Just as some birds can mimic human words, so some men can mimic God's words. If you are not truly moved and purely affected, or do not feel such gracious working within you, as you desire, remember that God will pour His Spirit on flesh; God will pour waters on dry ground; God will soften hard hearts. Even though we find no inclination within ourselves, the Lord will send floods of water instead of dryness, softness instead of hardness, and comfort instead of heaviness.

Now follows the third thing, that is, this *benefit* shall universally be poured out upon all. This highlights the goodness of God in giving it, as He does so without respect for persons, as much for children as for fathers, for servants as for masters, for women as for men, for the young as for the old. Along with this is the fourth thing, that this heavenly gift shall be poured out in a plentiful measure; in that, sons and daughters shall prophesy, young men shall see visions, and old men shall dream dreams. In this, we observe first the difference between the Law and the Gospel, between the fathers under the Law and those under the Gospel. We acknowledge that all had the same essence of faith and repentance; only, they looked for Christ to come, and we look to Christ already come. Here we must note two other differences: the first, that then the Spirit was given to a few, now it is given to many and all nations; then to one gender more specially, now to both; the other is that they had knowledge, but now they have more and a greater measure of both knowledge and repentance. For "young men shall see visions, and old men shall dream dreams." This, I say, is the first difference: that this grace is offered to more nations. For the first was bestowed only upon the Jews, for they alone had the Law, but now all is one; Christ is the head of both Jew and Gentile; there is one shepherd and one sheepfold for both Jew and Gentile (Psalm 147:19). The second note of difference is that the young men should see visions, and the old men dream dreams. This is a significant benefit and a unique sign of God's love for His people, that some of them should see visions, and some should dream dreams. It is said, "If there be a prophet among you, I the LORD will make myself known unto him in a vision, and will speak unto him in a dream," (Numbers 12:6). Although then some did prophesy, some did see visions, some did dream; yet now all shall prophesy, all shall see visions, all shall dream dreams: not that all shall be Prophets, as the Anabaptists and Family of Love do gather, but that now sons and daughters, servants, and women should have as great knowledge as those who among the Jews were chosen Prophets.

Now that it cannot be literally understood (and there is great danger if it is not rightly understood), it is proved in this way: because there was never any age at one time in which all were Prophets, yet this saying was true and fulfilled in the Apostles' time. Still, not so literally that we can perceive that all the Apostles prophesied and saw dreams. Peter and Paul indeed saw dreams, but where shall we find that all the other Apostles did so? Yet this was not so fulfilled unless the hearers also should prophesy. But this was not so even at that time, so it must not have been literally fulfilled in them, that all sorts of men had all these gifts. It must necessarily follow that it was never so universally fulfilled, either at that time or ever, for even in the Apostles' time, all were not Teachers, nor shall it ever be so, because God is a God of order, not confusion, and has appointed and purposed this diversity, that some should be Teachers and some learners. Therefore, the Apostle, after he has laid down the various callings of Christians for the edification of the Church (1 Corinthians 12), adds in verse 29, "Are all apostles? Are all prophets? Are all teachers?" Even Paul proves that it was not so then. For as there are diverse members in one body, and all members do not have the same office, so it is in the Church of Christ. Not all are Prophets; not all are Apostles; not all are Teachers. As if he should say: We see it is not so, but God has otherwise disposed it. In Ephesians 4, it is said that Christ, when He ascended, did ordain various offices, some to be Apostles, and some Prophets, and some Evangelists, and some Pastors and Teachers, for gathering together the saints for the work of the ministry, and for the edification of the body of Christ, until the number of the elect be fulfilled, and not until men become perfect in this life, as some have foolishly dreamed. Here we see some teachers, and the rest the work of the ministry. Again, Paul in his Epistle to the Philippians titles his epistle to the Saints, which was the Church, and to the bishops and deacons, the two orders of teachers, as pastors and teachers, so that now as then, some are teachers and some are not. Here, it is evident that as some then were teachers and some not, so it is now, for he speaks not only to the Church at Philippi, but to all Churches. If there be any at this day who will not be satisfied with the Scripture, but want the Saints' writings, I have already proven with St. Augustine, St. Chrysostom, and others. Therefore, we conclude that God will fulfill this prophecy in His Church, though not all shall be Prophets, not all teachers, not all speakers, yet all the saints shall have knowledge, and not all the same measure, for some are but babes, some young men, and some fathers in Christ.

There may also be another argument why this passage should not be understood literally, and that is drawn from the interpretation of similar passages in Scripture. In Exodus 19, Moses tells the people that the Lord has called them to be Kings, Priests, and Prophets. This is repeated by the Apostle Peter in the New Testament, and by John in the Apocalypse, and is applied, as in this place, generally to all Christians. Now the Jews never thought that every man was a King, sitting on a throne, thereby overthrowing the political state. They did not think that every man was a Priest, assuming that office upon himself, but that they had the liberty of their consciences and were freed from the bondage of men and sin. Also, through Christ, they might offer up first their prayers, then their souls and bodies to be a holy and acceptable sacrifice to Him. Neither do we, at this day, think any differently about the kingly priesthood of Christians. So why then should we think grossly and literally that indeed we have become Prophets with that special calling, and thus take away the order of Teachers and learners that God has ordained? For as we are Priests, so we are Prophets. If the speech must be qualified in one, why ought it not to be so in the other?

Again, we say of prophecies as we say of miracles. Before the word was written, the Lord taught His people by visions and dreams, and to prepare them to receive His doctrine and confirm them in it, He both worked miracles Himself and gave power to others to do so, as we may see in Moses, Elijah, and Elisha. He gave power to do miracles when the Law was written because the Gospel was not yet revealed; and when the Gospel was revealed, He continued His gift, because the Holy Spirit was not yet given. Even when the Spirit was poured out upon the Apostles, this gift remained in the Church, for the Spirit had not yet gained credit. But when the Gospel was revealed, the Spirit sent down and confirmed by signs and wonders, the use of miracles ceased. Not that there are no miracles at all now (for we do not shorten the hands of the Lord), but they are few and extraordinary.

Now the rules by which we shall test whether they are from God are these: if they either convert and win men to the word or confirm those already won in the word; if they agree with the word and carry the same majesty as the word, then they may be received as from God. But when they do not agree with these rules, though the thing done is miraculous, they are much to be suspected, as the miracles of old were received with reverence. For God, in His secret judgment, sometimes allows such to be done so that the wicked and unbelievers may be more effectively deluded. We also know that the Antichrist comes with signs, and they are so effective that even the very elect, if possible, would be deceived by them.

Similarly, we say of dreams and visions, until the Gospel came and gained credit in the hearts of men, there were visions and prophecies of things to come. But since these have now *ceased*, it is not ordinary that the Lord should make all Prophets or teach by visions and dreams. Why do we spend more time proving that this place cannot be understood as the words at first might seem to indicate, especially since the devilish opponents of both Papists and the Family of Love are so gross and palpable on this point?

The Spirit of these men is such, and so contrary to the good spirit of God, that where Scripture should simply be interpreted without any metaphor or allegory, they turn it into allegories, as we see many places perverted by the Papists, and almost the whole Scriptures by the Family of Love. On the other hand, where Scripture, by comparing places, shows that it should be understood metaphorically, they stick bluntly to the literal words, as in the words "*Hoc est corpus meum.*" The Papists would have no metaphor here, yet the whole course of Scripture enforces it. The Family of Love will admit the natural sense in almost no place, yet here they insist on the word, despite all the previous reasons.

This surely happens by God's righteous judgment, since they would neither acknowledge nor yield to the natural sense when they could; therefore, they cannot see where a metaphor should be applied. Thus it was with their great master of allegories, Origen, who, following his devised allegories, could not see through God's righteous and just judgment those places that would allow a metaphor. In his literal interpretation of Christ's saying about three kinds of chaste persons, where one makes himself chaste for the kingdom of God's sake, he misunderstood it so grossly that he cut off his own members.

The true understanding of this place, then, is that in the Apostles' times and the ages following, there should be more mature knowledge than was in the ages before. But if it's objected that men of our days are not like the great men and Prophets of God, such as Elijah, David, Jeremiah, or Daniel, we answer that comparisons must be made in like terms. If we compare the Apostles with the Prophets that were before them, we know that the Apostles surpassed them in clarity and excellence of knowledge. Our Savior Christ testifies of John the Baptist that he was the greatest among the Prophets, and yet the apostles and ministers of the Gospel were greater than he.

Then, compare our evangelists with the patriarchs, and they saw a clearer light than these did. For Abraham saw Christ from afar and yet to come, while they saw Him evidently and already come. Proceed to compare the common sort of people then with the common sort now, and even we see Christ more vividly portrayed before us than they did. They had assurance that these things would come to pass; we know that they have already come to pass, clearly seeing the effects and results.

And in this way we see that God's graces are more numerous and more excellent than they were in the time of the Law. Compare Christ with Moses, and He far exceeded him, just as the master builder surpasses the hired servant. Compare the common ministers of the Law, the Priests and Levites, with our ordinary Doctors and Pastors, and they excel them in the clarity of knowledge. All those notable men of the Law knew that Christ and the Holy Ghost would come, but the manner of their coming they saw only darkly; we see it and rejoice in it.

The plain meaning of this place is that whereas God revealed His will to some by visions and dreams in the old times, now all sorts of people, young and old, men and women, will be instructed in the knowledge of God more abundantly and more perfectly. It must be understood as in Exodus 19, "You shall be a kingly priesthood," and 1 Peter 2, and interpreted as in Isaiah (chapter 11), Jeremiah, and in the Gospel according to John, where it is said, "They shall all be taught of God."

The Spirit of Christ and the Spirit of prophecy are all one, and this is that which should possess the hearts of all men and teach them. It shall be an inward and invisible schoolmaster, teaching us to avoid what is evil and to do what is good. It's not only our duty to have Christ in our mouths but in our hearts, that we may know Him and have fellowship with Him, that we may grow in grace and in the knowledge of Him, so we may be partakers of His divine nature, and have assurance of

His love and favor towards us. But we should not take that as an occasion to cast off the external means, the reading, and preaching of God's word, and meditation upon it, but as a means to work through it more effectually. This is the true meaning of the Prophet in this place.

Let's further understand what it means that men shall prophesy, that is, they will be taught by the Spirit of God in the word to test themselves, to examine the spirits of their teachers, to teach others, and to be capable of giving a reason for their hope before their enemies. For just as the Holy Spirit came upon Christ, it must come upon every one of His members, and just as He was anointed a Prophet, so His members must also be prophets. This sound knowledge consists of four things.

The first thing required in a Christian is that he be able to test himself and his standing before God, whether he is in the faith or not, whether he is a child of God or not, contrary to the doctrine of the Papists, and lukewarm Protestants, who rely only on common injunctions and customary practices. Therefore, Paul charges the entire Church of Corinth, "Examine yourselves, whether ye be in the faith or no," (2 Corinthians 12) and to this, he adds a fearful warning, "unless you are refuse." Whoever is not in the faith is refuse, and if a man does not know whether he is in the faith or not, then he does not know whether he is in Christ or not. This examination must be according to the Scriptures, for our Savior Jesus Christ says, "Search the Scriptures, for they testify of me," and in another place, He says, "Ye err, because ye know not the Scripture," (John 5:39). Then we must not rely on the Preacher, or on this or that man, but we must believe because we have found it in the Scripture and have been taught it by the Spirit, as the men of Samaria said to the woman when she told them of Christ.

Moreover, we must not merely and superficially know the Scriptures but apply them to our personal use, and make our own faith certain by them if we are not reprobates. This is the first thing required of Christians. The second thing is that we be able to test our Teachers, not in everything they speak, but in matters pertinent to salvation. We are commanded to do this in 1 Corinthians 5, Ephesians 4, and in the Epistle of Saint John, "Try the spirits, whether they be of God or no," and in the epistles of Peter and Jude, it is said that those were perverted with heresies, never coming to know the truth, unstable, and carried away with every wind of vain doctrine. Therefore, we must not be always learning and yet never come to the knowledge of the truth. The truth must dwell richly in us with all wisdom, so we may discern the spirits. When we have weighed and found anything according to the word, then we must receive it as the word of God with reverence. If we find anything false in it, we must be far from accepting it; we must consider accursed the one who brings it, even if he were an Angel from Heaven. Foolish, then, is the frantic fantasy of the

Family of Love, which will say, "We may not judge, we cannot condemn." Every Christian taught by the Spirit may, indeed must, in the liberty of the Spirit, test and condemn all that is not in harmony with the holy word of God.

The third thing required of a Christian is that, through his knowledge, he be able to instruct and admonish others. Jude requires this in his epistle, that we should edify one another in our most holy faith (Jude 1:20). This is also given as a charge in Hebrews 3 that we should admonish one another, and in Hebrews 5, it is said that we ought to be teachers by now. Our Savior Christ also commands us that if our brother offends, we should admonish him. We owe this duty, and we must be capable of performing it, especially to those of our household, town, kin, and gradually to all people, as we have occasion to deal with them and as our calling permits us.

The fourth thing is that we should be able to give an account of our hope, even to our enemies. Peter requires this in plain words (1 Peter 3:15); our Savior Christ requires it, that if we would have Him confess us before His Father, we should confess Him before men (Matthew 10:32). These things were fulfilled in the Apostles' times, in the early Church, and in Queen Mary's days, and this can be found even among us in many places. Therefore, this is the true and natural meaning of this place.

This was never found in the Anabaptists, who were more honest the younger they were in heresy. If they grow old in their heresy, they do not grow so much in knowledge as in subtlety to invent human phrases, to deceive with newly concocted terms. They will not confess anything before a Magistrate. If they are caught, they will recant; if they die, they will say it is for the truth. Therefore, take heed of them.

There is some question here about the timing. Some understand it to mean Christ's coming in the flesh; some, His coming to judgment. Others, more accurately, think it refers to the entire time between His coming in the flesh and His coming to judgment. This seems the most probable opinion, both based on what has been said before and what follows after. For in the words preceding, it is said, "In the last days I will pour out my Spirit." Now the giving of the Spirit was fulfilled during that whole time spoken of. Moreover, the part that follows concerning calling upon the name of the Lord refers to that time as well. If both what precedes and what follows are understood to be of that time, then it is probable that what is in the middle is likewise understood in that way. And although Christ's first coming was a glorious time, as we can see from the Apostle's testimony, His last coming will be a far more glorious day; as we can see in Titus 2, 2 Thessalonians 4, where His coming is described to be with angels and with a shout. Yet, because this glory appears throughout the whole course of redemption, it is good to understand this as referring to the entire time, during all of which He does not cease to offer these graces and to execute these judgments.

As for the words themselves, some think they should be understood literally; some allegorically and spiritually. But they admit both interpretations. First, in their natural meaning, it is apparent because the Lord never leaves His Church without some instructions in the Sun, the Moon, the Heavens, and the Earth. Besides natural eclipses in the Sun and Moon and other exaltations, there have been extraordinary works in both that have been seen as signs of God's wrath for sin. Furthermore, we can confidently deduce that there was never any strange eclipse, comet, appearance in the heavens, shaking of the earth, strange and unnatural births; but after this change in nature, some event came strangely sooner or later. This showed that men had broken their obedience to God and had become monstrously disobedient, which the Lord makes known to us by altering the course of nature. Therefore, we say that before significant earthquakes, plagues, wars, comets, famine, or the like, comes great contempt for religion, monstrous profanity: so they become the signs of some notable sins either in religion, in life, or in both. Therefore, we neither exclude the literal sense, nor do we accept the fancy, or rather frenzy, of the Family of Love, because we acknowledge that after strange disobedience and contempt follow strange punishments and revenge. So, the Prophet shows the works of God for sin, either by what follows or by the signs that precede. Why, at this time when He would show Himself so gracious, should the Lord send such tokens of His wrath? Here we see a teaching contrary to our human nature, because God wants His mercy manifested when He shows His justice. And since men, hearing of the Gospel, imagine worldly happiness, Peter, to awaken them from this dream, helps them understand that unless these gifts are received reverently, God will be most angry, because they either refuse or abuse the mercies of God so offered. The use of this is partly concerning the elect and regenerated people and partly concerning the wicked and unregenerate. Regarding the elect, either before or after their regeneration; before their regeneration, it brings them to seek Jesus Christ. For though it is certain that God will call those He has predestinated and chosen in time, since His Gospel is not as precious to them as it should be, the Lord sends them crosses, sometimes poverty, sometimes sickness, sometimes reproach, sometimes a troubled mind, sometimes private misery, and sometimes public calamity to involve them among others. This is because they have no more trust in God's promises before they are humbled. Since men will not be easily or usually humbled by the mere word, the Lord seals it by sending troubles. When we can feel no comfort either in heaven or on earth, but perdition and cause for damnation within ourselves, we should then be more fit to receive comfort in Christ.

Again, since God's children have one particular fault or another, such as secret pride, vainglory, self-love, or other hidden corruptions, and the word of God cannot be allowed to draw us out of these sins, the Lord sends affliction. Through His correction, He draws us out of our worldly righteousness and makes us conscious of inward and hidden corruptions. He reminds us through misery that the same corruption lurking in others dwelt naturally in us, though repressed by God's hand, it did not violently burst forth. Where others lie in sin and do not know it, because natural light is suppressed within them, and God's Spirit can hardly work upon them, the Lord brings them to recognize unknown sin and to make a conscience of known sin. He visits us with private and public means, so that, as the wicked will be endlessly tormented in hell without hope or relief, the merciful should have their hearts broken in mercy and measure. Because they would not do so through loving invocation and invitation by the Lord, it is done through crosses.

Secondly, it concerns the regenerate either to continue them in their good state or to keep them from gross sins. For God's children sometimes fall and always may fall if God does not keep them. Since David and Manasseh had sinned, God sent them the cross so that they might not forget Him. Because the same may be in us, if the Lord will pour out His wrath upon the wicked, surely He will not allow His children to go unchecked. We must not, as some are wont to do, say, "Did not David sin, make much of me, was not David a great sinner and yet saved?" It would indeed be good if we would bind David's sin with David's repentance, or if we consider how the Sun was turned into darkness, and the Moon into blood in his kingdom; if we see the pillars of God's judgments and vapors of His wrath against him among his own, how his sons rebelled, they who wanted to be counselors became traitors, and how the wicked villains triumphed over him; we would surely know that it does little good to tally up David's sinning. God does this to silence the wicked, so they cannot say that God spares and does not punish sin in His own, and that they should not dream of escape when His own servants are so chastened. Although God's children do not presently fall but are ready to fall, He often wraps them in the wicked's crosses, not so much to punish any present sin, but to prevent some future sin, by taking away the occasion of sinning, that He might humble them before they fall.

Again, although they are not subject to gross sins, yet because they are often puffed up with secret pride, become dead, unmerciful, dull, forsaking their first love, sometimes neither hot nor cold, lukewarm, without zeal—in short, they are not as God's children should be or as they themselves sometimes have been—the Lord in wisdom corrects these deficiencies and infirmities so that from infirmities they do not burst into enormities; from sinning in general, they do not fall into particular sins. Therefore, when the sun is darkened and the moon turned to blood, and such tokens of God's wrath are seen among the wicked, God's children should look at these as mirrors of their deformity. They should see what sin is in the wicked, and if it is so ugly, what it is in themselves. They should labor not to sin when God's hand is heavy on them.

In conclusion, we must observe what becomes of the wicked. Surely, if God's children receive so many crosses to bring them to heaven, those who receive none, who can feel no comfort in heaven or earth, no hand, no voice, but their own hearts, must be most wretched. Indeed, they are twice wretched. First, because God does not correct them, nor did He ever intend to correct them, but determined to give them over to a reprobate mind and let them ripen in sin that they might be the fitter for damnation. Secondly, because they think themselves happy, not feeling God's hand; for surely their reward will be according to their work, and they will have their portion with the wicked. For the fire that burned Sodom is the very fire that will burn all the wicked and ungodly. If then the Lord reserves the wicked for the day of judgment to be punished, and if these judgments against the wicked should be as sure as if they had already taken place, then let the wicked know, unless they repent and are converted, they will surely die the death.

Is this the Gospel that you profess? Look at the turmoil, look at how many opinions there are, what a variety of religions have arisen, look at what denial of the faith, what grave sins have emerged, look at what deaths, plagues, and wars are associated with it? Surely it seems that this is not the Gospel. Before, everything was in a better state; there was no such disturbance in religion, no such noise of notorious sins, no such tumult on every side; everything was at peace. But now we have more troubles than were ever heard of in earlier times. The wicked do not only break their necks at this obstacle, but even God's own children have dangerously stumbled at it. For when Job, David, and Jeremiah, without God's spirit, observed the prosperity of the wicked and the adversity of the godly, they confessed their feet had almost slipped, except that they dared not condemn the generation of God's children.

To remedy this, the Holy Spirit says that, when God's graces appear most, then will the Lord send the greatest judgments for the *contempt* of His Gospel in the wicked, and for the neglect of it in the godly. Now this is foretold so that we might not be offended when it comes; and this use does Christ teach us to make of it, "These things have I told you before, that when they come to pass," *etc.* (John 14:29). For to God's children, being but babes in Christ, this is a great temptation.

And to come to our days: Is it not troubling to many that there are so many *unlearned* ministers, and of learned ministers that there are so many *ungodly* men, that they see such oppressive Magistrates, such rebellious people, such careless governors, that there is such a height of subtlety in covering and cloaking sin; where there is the most knowledge, such running to sin; where there is the most preaching, and where the Gospel is received, that there should be such sects and heresies; when they shall see the Papists ready to defy the Gospel, what may a man do now, or how may he steady himself, if the Lord should leave him? Surely God has foretold it.

Even as the sun then shining bright, the moon giving light, the clear air are tokens of God's love, so much more the word: and as these being darkened and obscured show God's wrath; so the word obscured does testify His wrath much more. Indeed, if famines, plagues, or such like come, we must be forewarned of them. And our Savior Christ, when men asked Him for signs, He told them of many (Matthew 24), that there would be such wonders in the heavens, in the earth, and in the seas, that even the very elect would be nearly confounded.

Now, if Christ had not forewarned these things in the fairness of His judgment, we might indeed have had some cause for offense. And for this reason, our Savior Christ says, "Blessed are they that are not offended in me," (Matthew 11:6), because such confusions shall be, that men will be ready to lay the blame for these things on the Gospel and on the word:

and therefore blessed are they, that are forewarned of these things, and know why they come.

If the Jews would not hear the Apostles speaking the truth, was it any wonder if they were seduced by false teachers? If men do not receive the word in love, is it any wonder if they are deluded with heresy (2 Thessalonians 1)? If men neglect the peace of their minds offered by the Gospel preached, is it any wonder if they have wars? If men neglect the food of their souls, is it any wonder if they find a famine?

When we see then that men turn the Gospel into wantonness and write against it, is it a wonder if the Lord sends troubles? No, no, when men shall see such confusion, let them know that God *will* clear His justice, and recompense vengeance to the wicked, and restore the godly to their joys; and yet show them that here is no place of rest, but that they must lift up their heads to heaven, where they shall have rest without trouble.

Now let us consider what these afflictions work in the wicked, and to what end they are sent to them. Surely to plague them, and to leave them without excuse. They are sent to God's children to humble them, to bring them to repentance, to keep them from evil, to encourage them in good, and to recover them if fallen. But they are sent to root out the wicked, and to consume them from the face of the earth: and therefore, He pours out all the vials of His wrath upon the wicked remnant. And these manifold plagues have often come to pass where the Gospel has been preached because, as it is the greatest mercy and treasure if it is received, so the unnatural refusal of it does cause the greatest judgments. Thus, the Israelites in the wilderness were punished, first by idolatry, then by plagues, and were rooted out of the land. And after Christ had spoken, the Apostles preached, and the Jews remained unprofitable, the Lord, in His justice, in that they would not believe the true Christ, allowed them to be deluded by false Christs, and that they who would not profit by the true Apostles should be deceived by false Apostles, and then, being punished with famine and sickness, they were by the Romans subdued.

When the Gospel came to be preached among the Gentiles, and was scorned, the Lord first punished them by allowing them to fall into vile sins, and then after gave them over to the Turk. We see how in the West country, where the Gospel was preached and refused, the Pope was sent to them. So likewise, must we benefit from this. When God's Spirit falls plentifully in us, and yet men by His word will not be reformed, the Lord will send heretics and wicked men to corrupt them. And will the Lord thus judge His own people, and will He spare the wicked? No, when we think all is quiet, the Lord will send plagues for refusing the health of our souls; the Lord will send famines for refusing the food of our souls; the Lord will plague us with wars for neglecting the peace of our minds. And (Matthew 24) the Lord has set Jerusalem as a type, in that the Gospel never continued quiet or uncorrupt in any one place for more than the space of a hundred years.

Well, if we do not see the beginnings of these things, we are half mad; if we will not fear the outcomes of them, we are worse than so; if we will not profit by these things, woeful experience will teach us our miserable state. We see how necessary affliction is in the godly, we see how profitable, we see how God does preserve His own, we see how He clears His justice upon the wicked.

It is of great concern, and not to be omitted, that these terrible judgments follow the Gospel, and that not casually or accidentally, but by necessity. For the word is God's candle, which reveals all secret sins, which are brought to light; and the world will not endure this, and so they are tormented and plagued. Secondly, the word is the key of heaven, and shuts up the wicked, and opens to the godly; this is most intolerable to the wicked, who therefore rise up against it. Thirdly, the word is a sword, which cuts and wounds the wicked, and pierces their consciences, though not unto repentance. Fourthly, the word does aggravate and increase sin, because men, hearing it and not profiting by it, have their consciences burdened more heavily. Fifthly, the word is a net, which catches the wicked, so that they are entangled in it, as Pharaoh in the Red Sea; and therefore, they are more and more burdened and plagued. And therefore, we conclude, that this wicked world cannot endure the Gospel, nor the Gospel it, but the word must root out the wicked, or the wicked the word, and therefore plagues follow it.

Therefore, if the Lord be true, as He is, surely great troubles are toward us, if we do not repent. Therefore, we are to be exhorted that as we have received the word in joy, we would not fall away in trouble. For as we have had comfort in the word, so we must have sufferings for it, and therefore He that has promised us the crown has also told us of the cross.

Let us pray therefore that the Lord would fit us for these plagues, and especially for the spiritual plagues; that we may have strength to stand in the evil day; that our garments may be made white in the blood of the Lamb; and that being clothed with Christ, we may endure all things in Him; and that when Christ shall appear, we may appear with Him in glory.

A Brief Treatise on Prayer

"And it shall come to pass, that whosoever shall call on the name of the Lord shall be saved," (Acts 2:21, cf. Joel 2:32).

By calling on the name of God in this context, which represents only one specific part of God's worship, the other aspects of God's worship are meant and understood. The Scriptures sometimes attribute other aspects of God's worship to this one part, such as in Genesis 3, when people began to call on the name of the Lord, and in Genesis 12, when Abraham built an altar and called on the name of the Lord, meaning he worshiped God. Again, in Psalm 50, "Call upon me in the time of trouble, and I will hear you." In the New Testament, we find the same. This passage is referred to in Romans 10 and 1 Corinthians 1, where the Apostle wishes grace to all those who call on the name of God, that is, worship God. In 2 Timothy 2, whoever calls on the name of the Lord, meaning worships God, must turn away from iniquity. So, under this one aspect of invocation, we understand *all* other parts. In our English language, we more often use phrases in conjunction with a worship service like, "We will go to prayers," or, "Are prayers done," rather than referring to going to hear the word of God, receive the Sacraments, and the like, even though we engage in other religious activities in the congregation besides prayer. Both Jeremiah and our

Savior Christ refer to the Church as a house of prayer, as in Matthew 21:13: "Mine house shall be called the house of prayer," *etc.* It is a place for hearing the word, receiving the Sacraments, executing discipline, as well as prayer, but this one name encompasses all.

Now, before we explain the reason for this, why is it that few people care for the word, fewer for the Sacraments, and even fewer for discipline, yet everyone appears to be friends to prayer? Even heretics, who will differ from us in other matters, will acknowledge prayer? This is a sign of God's goodness that no one abandons prayer. That by prayer, all parts of God's worship are meant, is evident in Matthew 24:13, where our Savior Christ says: "But he that endureth unto the end, he shall be saved." The means to avoid these judgments follow: The Gospel of the kingdom must be preached to all nations. In John 3, Christ must be lifted up through the preaching of the Gospel so that whoever listens to the word may be saved. These ideas are connected in Romans 10, where it's said, "Whoever calls on the name of the Lord, he shall be saved," and then, "But how shall they call on him, on whom they have not believed? And how shall they believe, unless they hear?" So, just as faith saves, faith comes by the word of God. In Ecclesiastes 4:17 and 5:1: "When you enter the house of God, look to your feet," etc. In this context, the Holy Spirit first teaches people to hear, then to pray, as they come to the Temple both to pray and to hear. Likewise, in Psalm 95, the Prophet first exhorts to prayer: "O come let us worship and kneel down," then mentions the word: "Today if you will hear his voice, harden not your hearts," because these two must be joined together. That the Ministers of God are required to attend to both, the Scriptures show, such as Deuteronomy 33, where the Levites' duty is first to teach Jacob and then to offer incense, meaning to pray, as seen in Psalm 141 and 2 Samuel 12, where the people, acknowledging their sins, request Samuel to pray for them. He answers them that he will not only pray to God for them but also preach God's word, threaten God's judgments, and proclaim God's mercies if they repent. In Acts 6, when the Apostles found themselves burdened with ordinary ministry duties, they established new means, and they committed themselves to the word and prayer. In 1 Timothy 1 and 2, Paul teaches Timothy first how he should preach to the people, then how he should pray for them, and so the Lord wants the people to come to hear the word preached as well as to pray. We will better understand this if we consider what the Lord requires of us in praying. Firstly, a man cannot be heard unless he does the will of God. As stated in Matthew 7: "Not every one, that says to me Lord, Lord, shall enter into the kingdom of heaven, but he that does the will of my Father that is in heaven." In Matthew 15:8,9: "This people draws near to me with their mouth, etc. But in vain do they worship me, teaching for doctrine men's precepts." Psalm 145:18: "The Lord is near to all that call upon him, yes, to all that call upon him in truth."

Proverbs teaches that the sacrifices and prayer of the wicked are sinful and an abomination to the Lord. In Psalm 34:15,16: "The eyes of the Lord are upon the righteous, and his ears open to their cry; but the face of the Lord is against them that do evil." Isaiah 59, "Your hands are defiled with blood, your lips with iniquity, your tongues have spoken lies, your lips have murmured wickedness. When you spread forth your hands, I will hide my eyes from you. When you make many prayers, I will not hear." John 9:31, "Now we know that God does not hear sinners." Proverbs 15:8, "The sacrifice of the wicked is an abomination to the Lord, but the prayer of the righteous is his delight." The publicans and Pharisees, both in their common prayer, were rejected, the one for his pride, the other for his injustice. We find this doctrine of not being heard for sin in Jeremiah 14 and 15. We must amend our lives, else our prayers are to no purpose, as shown in 1 Peter 3:7. We must give up our sins; the Psalmist teaches: "If I regard iniquity in my heart, the Lord will not hear me." In James 4:3, "You ask and receive not, because you ask amiss, to consume it upon your lusts." Without hearing *the word*, we cannot amend our lives. So, it is *vain* to pray without *hearing and obeying* the word. It is by the preaching of the word that men are brought to faith and repentance, so they may pray aright. Therefore, we conclude that both are necessary.

It is a small thing to lend the ears in hearing; it is easy to satisfy our delight with listening to a man renewing our knowledge. But to put to work the eye, the ear, the hands, to labor with the heart to set the whole body in a framework of subjection, as befits those who pray to the Lord (which shows that prayer is a thing both painful and laborious), we will find it to be a very difficult thing. Prayer brings the experience of the things which we know, and without it, we have as little proof of our knowledge as those who have no use of a hidden treasure and never benefit from it. The word makes known to us the treasures of God's wisdom, but faith brings the experience of them by applying and appropriating these mercies of God to ourselves, and prayer is the instrument by which this faith is sustained in us. The word tells us that God will plague sinners; prayer brings an experience of this. The word tells us that God cares for us; prayer proves this. The word shows that the Lord has both power and mercy to show to His people; prayer obtains the trial of this. The word reveals to us the wisdom, providence, majesty, and goodness of God; prayer conveys the certainty of these things into us. God will be glorified wholly and only, and cannot tolerate that we should be partners with Him in this. If a man comes by knowledge, faith, and repentance by hearing, it is more of an infusion into a man than an action from a man, and it is God's great mercy. But when the Lord brings a man to his knees and humbles him in prayer and compels him to ask all of God, that we might hear rightly and use the things heard, this breaks a man's heart and makes him say, "Great is the Lord." This, I say, humbles a man to acknowledge his needs; this calls down many blessings, both spiritual and corporeal, from the Lord. We know that although a father is ready and fully intends to leave an inheritance to his children, yet to acquaint them with obedience, he will have them ask things of far lesser value at his hands. Likewise, God, although He has purposed to give us a heavenly inheritance, which in Christ is purchased, yet to continue us in faith and obedience, He will have us ask it of Him. If human wisdom can come this far, should we not thereby gather the wisdom of God? If a man has this pity, should we doubt mercy in God? And as prayer brings experience of God's love, so it also proves our knowledge, faith, and repentance. For if we are to be suitors at God's hand, we must not willingly displease Him. We see that when we would obtain a favor from a man, we will be careful not to offend him, unless we should suffer refusal. Likewise, when we pray, we must prepare our hearts for obedience, and therefore the Scripture speaks of cleansing our hearts of hypocrisy and faithlessness. If this care is taken in suits for things corruptible, that we will not willingly offend the one to whom we plead, then we must know that God is the Lord of spirits. To pray to Him without avoiding things that displease Him and without doing things that please Him is nothing but gross hypocrisy. Then the man who prays often must be a godly man, and if we are so bold to pray, nourishing sin in us, besides being dull in prayer, we are inwardly both accused and cursed. Therefore, comes such abundant acknowledgment of our sins in prayer, with a purpose to avoid them. Therefore, come such vows and declarations of obedience, so that prayer not only sustains repentance but also breeds thankfulness. For it is our corruption when we know that we obtained something in ways other than prayer, that we then attribute it to the means. But when we see God has heard our prayers, it seals our faith, it confirms our thankfulness. It is true that God gives many mercies without praying; yet this must make us more thankful and not deter us from using the means that God has appointed. That prayer further confirms love to God is already evident.

Now we must show how it works love even to our brethren. When a man comes to pray and is choked by the fact that he must forgive, or else not be forgiven, he must either be a hypocrite in his prayer, or cease from prayer, or forgive his enemies. It is blatant hypocrisy to desire God to forgive us many and great sins, and we will not pardon our brother a few and light offenses. If we take a view of the weight, height, length, depth, and breadth of our sins, we will confess it as hypocrisy to crave pardon for so many sins, being hardly brought to forgive others a few trespasses. And for this reason, the Scripture says, "If ye forgive not others, ye cannot be forgiven," (Matthew 6:15). If then *prayer* is such a thing as nature least entertains, if it brings such experience of God's love towards us, if it so confirms faith, continues repentance, and causes love both to God and man, it is good reason that this is set to bring about the other and make all other parts of God's worship more effective. He shall be saved. That is, in the midst of diseases he shall not be taken away, in the time of iniquity, he shall not be overtaken; but in all these, he shall suffer with Faith and a good conscience. Besides, by the word of saving, is meant the obtaining of all graces, as pledges of our salvation, and gauges of our inheritance, so that it does not simply signify an exemption from the former judgments threatened. Will a man then escape the wrath threatened and enjoy the grace promised? Let him use true and heartfelt prayer, which has its fruit commended to us both in the chapter going before, in the selection of the Apostles, and also at the beginning of this chapter, in that being gathered together in prayer, the Holy Ghost was sent down. Now let's speak a little of the circumstances. First, of the persons, it is said, "Whosoever." Secondly, regarding the extremity of the time, it is said, "shall be saved," that is, from those judgments and endowed with those graces, that even then, when there shall be so many opinions that we shall not be able to discern the truth well, when wickedness shall abound everywhere, examples of godliness are nowhere, when we shall be able to find no comfort either in ourselves or in others; we shall be so governed that we shall not only avoid evil but coldness in well-doing, and what is lost through the injuries of time shall be added in inward graces and recompensed in the kingdom of heaven. When we then in the extremity of offenses say,

"Good Lord, what shall we do? Where shall we go to hear a good Preacher? What may we do to go to some good man and zealous professor?" Remember then, if you will rely on the Lord, and resort to prayer, though you are troubled with Papists, or Heretics, or monstrous livers, then lean on God, trust in His word, and use prayer. When you shall see no good either in Church or in Commonwealth, then have recourse to prayers, there will you find a refuge, you shall obtain, and God will be honored.

And it will come to pass. This signifies the time of the Gospel, and here is shown a difference between the time of the Law and the time of the Gospel. If our fathers were heard under the Law, if they did not receive a rejection in the beginning of the day, what may we hope for under the Gospel? What confidence may we receive now when the sun shines out at its fullness? Whatever proof they had, we may have more; whatever experience they had, we may have it in a greater measure, because what they had confirmed, we have confirmed. The Lord requires of us now to trust in Him more, and we must remember that saying of our Savior Christ, "Hitherto have ye asked nothing in my Name, ask, and ye shall receive, that your joy may be full," (John 16:24). If our fathers prayed fervently, why do we not? Do we not have more deeds of God's favor? Do we not have more promises? Do we not have more examples? All of which accuse us of a lack of zeal in prayer. In the Old Testament, they did not name Christ; we are bold to look upon God in Christ, His Son. Woe then be to us if these things do not move us, seeing Christ stands on the right hand of God the Father, who is not now in the loins of Abraham, or in the womb of the Virgin, or in the bowels of the earth; but no, as if in heaven, we may see Him sitting on the right hand of God.

The circumstance remaining is in this word, "whosoever," which shows that whether it be man or woman, master or servant, young or old, Jew or Gentile, no age, no sex, no estate, no condition is excluded. It is true that there are privileges of the man above the woman, of the master above his servant, of the elders above the young; but this is in some things, not in all. For in the worship of God, in the matter of God's glory, and our salvation, there is no respect of persons with God; but whoever calls upon the name of the Lord, he shall be saved. In regard to this, we are to be exhorted, that if we will rejoice in this privilege, we must use the means due to those who are within the precincts of it, we must not excuse ourselves, and say; *I am a woman, and the weaker vessel, I am a young man and reckless, I am an old man and forgetful, I am a servant, and am not at my own liberty.* For if we look for the grace offered, we must use the means proposed.

But yet, there is more than this, that not only the righteous shall be saved, but also the poor sinner if now he will repent, and having a pure purpose to please God, call on the name of the Lord. Behold, O repenting sinner, the thief on the cross; the Sun was darkened, the veil of the Temple rent, earthquakes, and troubles, confusion was among men, terrors were in himself, and yet he, calling on the name of the Lord, and saying, "Lord, remember me when thou comest into thy kingdom," received this comfortable answer, "This day shalt thou be with me in Paradise."

Peter, seeing Christ, was pardoned. If we behold David's misery, in the troublesome state of both Church and Commonwealth, when he had not one of his own children to comfort him, but to increase his grief, one brother murdered another, one of his sons, being a traitor, was through God's judgment hanged by the hair of the head, his chief friends rebelled against him; he was not only in all this mightily preserved by God but also received plentiful graces of the Spirit. When Manasseh had caused Jerusalem to swim with blood when the city was near destruction, and he himself in chains; what hope was there either for the Kingdom or Prophecy to continue? And yet calling on God's name, he was heard and helped. If such great things were for poor sinners before Christ, what comfort is there for them since Christ has come? If the wretched man was so helped by Christ, even when he was on the cross; what comfort may afflicted consciences hope for in Him, being advanced to the Throne and Kingdom? No, I will add more, even very hypocrites by prayer have escaped outward perils, like Ahab, and such like. Yes, and mark those who are in wars or in some great distress, how praying to the Lord, they are helped. The same we shall observe sometimes either in worldlings or in God's children unregenerate. All of which will grant that after they have prayed, but in their manner, the Lord has strangely delivered them. If wicked men have had this benefit, how much more shall the godly have it? If God's children have found such grace before they knew God; what grace shall they have when they know Him, believe in Him, and call upon Him?

Here then is all doubting to be taken away, and we must cease to say: *Oh, I am a sinner, I cannot be helped, my unworthiness makes me ashamed.* Consider the tenor of this runs in a universal point to all; you cannot be excluded if you do not exclude yourself. And why? It is said that all shall be saved, which point is necessarily to be noted. For the devil will tell us, Christ died for others, but not for us. It is true that all repentant sinners, compared with the number of the unrepentant, are but few. Howbeit, if I truly abhor my sins, and myself for my sins' sake, if I purpose to leave sin and travel in the ways of righteousness, if I love God and hate iniquity and depart from it, although I lack all these solemn preparations, yet I am persuaded I shall be saved. And yet remember, that here is no such liberty for hard-hearted sinners; neither is the Sea of mercy denied to sorrowful sinners. For, as no sinner shall be damned that will repent, and in truth desire to be saved: so, the Lord will not justify the wicked and obstinate sinner.

Whosoever, therefore, has ears, let him hear, whoever has eyes, let him see, whoever has a heart, let him consider this bountiful mercy of God, whether he be in misery outward or trouble inward; and know from the Lord's own mouth that, "Whosoever calleth on the Name of the LORD, he shall be saved."

Directions for Consolation

Short rules sent by master Richard Greenham to a gentlewoman troubled in mind, for her direction and consolation. Also, this is very necessary for every Christian to be exercised with as it pertains to directions for walking a Christian life.

1. Temptations will be held against you if you give in to them. Therefore, do not yield, but resist, as St. James advises.
2. No thought will harm you unless you agree with it in your heart. You are not guilty of any sin that you wish to be free from in your heart; you lack no goodness that you desire in your heart (Romans 7).
3. When sickness is at its worst, there's hope it will lessen; the same goes for temptation.
4. It's a great mercy from God to recognize a temptation during the time of temptation.
5. When you wish to do or receive any good, present your efforts and actions as a sacrifice to God through Christ, asking God to send His Holy Spirit to sanctify His own sacrifice.
6. If you experience even a slight relief from temptation, give thanks, and you'll receive more.
7. It's as sinful to deny God's gifts as it is to be presumptuous about them.

8. A suppressed temptation, like a fire, burns more intensely within.
9. Always believe that you are in the presence of God and Christ and act accordingly.
10. Fear hidden sins more than public shame. Always believe that there's mercy with Jesus Christ.
11. Remember the past mercies you've received and consider your current state to be the same as God's children. If you're distressed, pray to God; if relieved, praise Him. There's a cycle of sorrow and comfort, just as there's day and night.
12. Avoid being discontent in any situation. Be content even if God denies your desires. If God doesn't answer your prayers, don't distress yourself too much. Don't intensely desire or be saddened by anything, except for gaining or losing God's *favor*.
13. Strive for humility and patience. Be willing to accept discipline and offer everything to God, from whom you received your life. If you resist, it will be like a bird in a trap; the more it struggles, the more trapped it becomes. Use the Word of God during troubles and temptations, like a sick person that eats food. Even if it feels unpleasant at first, it will benefit you in the end.
14. Patiently enduring suffering is a sacrifice pleasing to God. When a goldsmith places gold in fire to refine it, it might seem ruined to the

untrained eye. Similarly, God's children might seem ruined during afflictions to those who don't understand spiritual matters.

15. Always believe that your situation is God's doing, meant for your humility, comfort, God's glory, and the benefit of many.

16. Be cautious about frequently changing your opinion about your situation. Don't attribute it sometimes to God, sometimes to melancholy, sometimes to your own weaknesses, sometimes to witchcraft, and sometimes to Satan. These varying thoughts will trouble you. Recognize that melancholy might be a trigger, but not the root cause. Always focus on God's hand and trust that everything is for your good.

17. Don't say that you can't be helped, as it might hinder God's work. Don't think that being in a different place would make things better. God is everywhere, both where you are and where you wish to be.

18. If you fear not persevering to the end because many others have fallen away, remember that as long as you rely on yourself, you have reason to fear. But if you rely on God, you have only reasons for faith. Just as a person swimming in deep water is safe as long as their head is above water, you are safe in Christ, who is above all troubles.

19. Believe that God the Father oversees your temptations, the Holy Spirit assists you, Jesus Christ overcame temptations for you, and the saints on earth pray for you, even those who've never met you.
20. Only the light of the Spirit can judge the work of the Spirit, just as only the sun can judge itself.
21. Don't argue with God, or you'll be embarrassed. Don't argue with Satan, or you'll be defeated.
22. Always believe that your punishment is less than what your sins deserve.
23. In the midst of the many blessings you receive from God, don't be surprised if you also face challenges. God gives blessings with challenges to prevent despair and challenges with blessings to prevent arrogance.
24. For any external blessing you can't have, pray to God that you won't be upset about it.
25. No shame, grief, or sorrow pleases God if it's separated from the assurance of His favor. Likewise, being pleased with the assurance of forgiveness isn't acceptable to God if it ignores the importance of recognizing, lamenting, and avoiding sin. Always deal with your sins and condemn them to death. While you have a clear conscience and fear sin, ignore Satan's accusations and disregard the threats of hell.
26. Satan tries to blind some with false happiness to keep them from seeing their sins and to oppress

others with baseless fears to keep them from feeling the joy of redemption. He knows that joy can be temporarily interrupted but not permanently denied. So, he tries to reduce your rightful joy in Christ. By giving in to these fears, you diminish the effectiveness of your prayers and lose the joy of serving God.

27. A strict religious path might seem uncomfortable, but it's a blessing if it makes us *more like Christ*. Don't let your heart be restricted in spiritual matters. This can weaken your devotion. May the Lord protect you, bring you joy, grant you the spirit of prayer, and answer your prayers. Praying is the best way to serve God and the most comforting act you can do. I'm eager to remind you of these things. I care more for your soul than for my own well-being. It would be devastating for me to see your soul suffer. Let me be more than just a worldly friend. Allow me to be more than just a friend of the flesh.

FINIS

A Set of Wholesome Guidelines or Directions for a Christian Life

1. Don't think too highly of yourself. The humbler you see yourself, the more esteemed you are in God's eyes. God values a humble spirit, as the humble tax collector who recognized his own unworthiness was more favored by God than the proud Pharisee who bragged about himself.
2. Speak of God with reverence, recognizing that we aren't even worthy to utter His name, let alone use it carelessly.
3. Stay close to God in both good times and bad. In hard times, we turn to God, but in good times, we *often* forget Him. If you face adversity, don't lose hope but cling to God. He will deliver you when it seems impossible, for His glory and for the benefit of His children, just as He delivered Daniel from the lions.
4. Make up for past mistakes with repentance. Approach the present with diligence and the future with foresight.
5. Don't let anger or resentment cause you to reveal secrets that you once promised to keep.
6. Be discerning when giving praise, be polite when greeting others, and be kind and patient when offering advice, avoiding rashness and anger.

7. Read a portion of God's word every day. Ensure not only that you serve God sincerely but also that your household does the same.
8. Whatever blessings you ask from God, request them in the name of Christ. For Christ said, "No one comes to the Father except through me," (John 14:6).
9. Before undertaking any task, seek God's guidance to determine if it's right to do. If it's permissible, then proceed with a peaceful heart.
10. Ensure that your food, clothing, and leisure activities are necessary, appropriate, and moderate.
11. Beware of sins of presumption. Many assume God's mercy, but while He is merciful to those who repent, He won't show mercy to those who merely presume upon it.
12. Renounce worldly desires and turn to God. Loving the world is incompatible with loving God. Furthermore, don't cling to anything worldly that might pull you away from God. God desires your whole heart, not just a part of it.
13. Always be prepared for temptations. Those who follow Christ should expect temptations. If you overcome a temptation, don't assume you're free from future ones. This life is often described as a *Christian battle*.
14. If you face temptations and trials, it's a clear sign you belong to God. God disciplines every child

He accepts. Conversely, those without any trials likely belong to the devil, who has no need to tempt those he already controls.

15. Avoid all sins and strive to do your best. God will accept your efforts, even if they're imperfect, through Christ's perfection. Don't cling to any particular sins, as the devil can control a person through a single sin as easily as through many.
16. Ensure that your words come from a good spirit, not from selfish desires. If they come from selfish desires, God will reject them.
17. As God showers you with mercy and goodness, respond with increased obedience.
18. When tempted by the devil or his agents, rely on God's word for defense. The Word is like a double-edged sword, defending us and attacking our enemies.
19. Christ used scripture to repel the devil. He could have easily banished the devil with a mere breath, but He chose to use scripture to set an example for us. To better understand the scriptures, read them regularly, discuss them, understand their meanings, compare different passages, and pray for understanding.
20. Emulate those who are wiser and more experienced than you. Observe and learn from the wise, associate with honest people, and cherish the company of the godly.

FINIS

APPENDIX: A Marriage Contract

After prayer, he spoke as follows. That none of us might doubt whether there is just cause for this manner of our meeting or not upon a natural light in nature for marriage, we must recall even from the heathens that the light of nature taught them that a solemn promise was to be made between the parties that should be married, before they were to be joined in marriage. This was called the espousal, and therefore we would be more to blame if we should neglect such a good custom, especially being commended to God's chosen people, as we can infer from His words. For we read that the Lord God made a law concerning espoused persons, that if they were unfaithful to their bodies, they should be condemned as adulterers, just as well as the married parties. Mary was also betrothed to Joseph before the solemnizing of their marriage. The Church's practice stands with good reason, for the neglect of it leads many to be disappointed in their intended marriages, as some of them, through inconsistency, go back. It is also very fitting that they should receive instructions about the graces and duties required in this state, so that they may pray to the Lord and be prepared and made ready to be publicly presented to the congregation afterward.

As for the nature of this contract and espousal, although it is a degree below marriage, it is more than a determined purpose, even more than a simple promise. Just as someone who delivers the estate of his lands in writing (with all conditions agreed upon) is more bound to perform his bargain than one who has merely purposed or promised by word of mouth, even if the writings are not yet sealed, there is a greater necessity to stand by this contract of marriage than any other purpose or promise made privately. Having observed these things, I plan (as God shall give me grace) to provide some lessons on how you must prepare yourselves *to live in the state of marriage*. I will aid your memory by going first through the Articles of your faith, then through the Commandments, noting specific duties suitable for this purpose.

Concerning your belief in God the Father, you know, brethren, that you must believe in Him as the Creator of all things, and also the Governor and Preserver of the same. You must also understand that He created man in His image, giving him preeminence and governance over the woman to help the man in serving God. So, you must be even more careful not to be hindered from the Lord by your wife. Many people, while desiring marriage, are careful in discharging their duty as long as their hope is deferred, but after enjoying what they looked for, they become more negligent than before, greatly dishonoring God through their ingratitude. It may be the man's fault alone if he is not helped by his wife to grow in godliness. I believe that even Eve, in urging her husband Adam to eat the forbidden fruit, would have helped him recognize Satan's malicious enmity against them both if, according to the great measure of graces he received from the Lord, he had been more faithful in obeying God and had wisely rebuked his wife. Yet, even though the woman was the cause of sin, the force of sin leading to human corruption came through the man's sin. As the Apostle says in Romans 5, "As by one man (*meaning Adam*) sin entered into the world, and death by sin, and so death went over all men, for as much as all men have sinned," (Romans 5:12). So much more has the grace of God and the gift of grace through Jesus Christ abounded to many. In Genesis 3, we read that the eyes of the woman were not opened until the man had eaten the fruit, but as soon as he had, the eyes of both were opened, and they knew they had sinned. Therefore, I gather that a rebuke would have been more successful in converting her than her urging him to transgress would have been in leading him astray. I do not say this to excuse the woman, for I know the Lord was displeased with her, and for that reason, He has placed a special punishment upon her in the painful bearing of children.

But to show the great responsibility that lies upon the man to restrain the woman's corruption due to the authority God has given him over her, I want you (brother) to consider this diligently. And you, my sister, must benefit by recalling that one purpose of your creation is to glorify God by helping your husband. Therefore, be careful not to hinder him, causing trouble or vexing his heart, whereby he would be less fruitful in his calling. Instead, be cheerful towards him so that even if he has little comfort in all other things, he may find great cause to rejoice in you. Understand that while your husband is required to seek wisdom to govern you, the Lord also requires you to be subject to him. Remembering also that as God has enjoined you to be silent in the congregation, you must seek instruction from him in your private room.

Another aspect to consider in your belief is faith in God's providence. Mark well what I tell you, for it is special, and I know it will benefit you if God blesses it to you. If you are assured in your hearts that it was the Lord who, in His gracious providence, brought you together, you will be comforted against all troubles and hindrances that may arise against you. Satan's nature is to cause doubt between men and women, leading to trouble and strife. Doesn't the impatience of spirit, the murmuring, chiding, cursing, and unrest we see in many come from the lack of reverent persuasion that the Lord in His providence has joined them in this close bond and union? Therefore, my good brother and sister, mark this point diligently, as it shall be a comforting stay for both of you, whatever may happen contrary to what you expected. Whether it be any mismatch in your dispositions or natures or falling into sickness or diseases, remembering that it was the *Lord*'s doing, you can be more assured that it will end well if you remain constant in prayer, calling upon God the Father through faith in Jesus Christ. To prove to your hearts that the Lord has knit you together, consider that it must be the Lord who moved the hearts of your Christian parents to give their lawful consent and that God will give you greater assurance as you observe His dealings with you over time.

Now, as to your faith in Jesus Christ, understand that marriage is holy only to those whose hearts are sanctified by faith in His name. Even though God always approves His ordinance, it is nevertheless a curse to the wicked who lack this faith. Therefore, you must be careful to continue believing that Christ has died and risen for your justification, being sanctified daily by His Spirit to walk as becomes His glory. If you do this, the Lord will, by His Spirit, assist you in the doing of such duties as pertain to your calling and state in the faith of Jesus Christ.

Next, as to the Holy Spirit, the Lord will give you such illumination that you may know the truth and follow it to the end. You shall be daily taught by Him to do that which is pleasing in His sight, though you must always remember that your faith in the Trinity is of the utmost importance for fulfilling your duties. You must begin in the name of the Father, continue in the name of the Son, and end in the name of the Holy Ghost. This is an excellent rule for you, for it is according to God's own institution, being a point of your faith as you profess it in your Creed.

For your further assistance, take the Ten Commandments as a directory for your lives, using them in the following manner:

1. In the first, you must understand that you must love God with all your heart, soul, and strength, and consequently one another. You must not allow any enmity, jealousy, or discontentment to grow between you. Instead, your love must be of the same quality as your faith in God, a love that keeps itself pure, being jealous of itself. It is the chief grace of all, and without it, all your other graces will be worthless.

2. In the second, it requires you to worship God after the true manner, that he appoints in his word, teaches you so much, that you must nourish your life in this estate, by the practice of things by which he is worshipped and honored of us, namely, by hearing, and reading of his holy word, and by the use of the Sacraments. For the same that is stirred up and nourished by this means, is most pure and will longest endure; where fatherly love soon vanishes and fades away.

3. In the third you must keep your words and promises with all your might, not allowing Satan or any other occasion to cause a breach between you. Take heed that you do not swear rashly or in anger, for this leads to a breaking of God's commandments.

4. In the fourth, remember to keep the Sabbath day holy. In your family, teach and instruct one another, exhorting and admonishing as need requires.
5. In the fifth, honor your parents, giving them thanks and doing your duties to them, even if they have been strict or severe towards you. For this is God's commandment, and He will surely bless you for your obedience.
6. In the sixth, take heed that you do not kill or wound one another, either in deed, word, or thought. Anger, envy, malice, hatred, and all such wickedness must be carefully avoided. Watch against them, and if at any time you fall into them, seek forgiveness from God and from each other.
7. In the seventh, be careful to preserve your chastity, being faithful to each other both in body and in mind. Do not lust after others, and avoid any appearance of evil.
8. In the eighth, do not steal from one another, whether in affection, goods, or anything else. Rather, give freely to each other, remembering that you are one flesh.
9. In the nineth, always speak the truth to each other, avoiding all deceit and lying.
10. In the tenth, do not desire or seek anything that belongs to others but be content with what God has given you. Be content with your condition,

whatever it may be, trusting in God's providence and care for you.

Following these commandments, as the rule of your lives, will lead you to live a godly, happy, and comfortable life. I shall pray to God that He may give you grace to follow these directions and instructions.

Let's end with a prayer.

O Most Merciful Father, who in thy wisdom hast appointed the estate of marriage for the comfort of mankind and the increase of thy Church with a godly seed, we beseech thee to assist these two thy servants with thy blessings, that they may faithfully perform the covenant they make before thee. Let thy Holy Spirit so guide and direct their hearts, that they may live together in love and peace all the days of their life. Grant that they may be fruitful in children, and that they may bring them up in thy fear and nurture. Let thy providence so order all things concerning them that they may serve thee with a cheerful heart, and when they shall have finished their course here on earth, grant them a place in thy heavenly kingdom. This we ask for Jesus Christ's sake, Amen.

After the exhortation and prayer, he asked the parties to be contracted these two questions:
1. Concerning their parents' consents. After their answer regarding their parents' consent, and to make a faithful promise of marriage to one another at such time as their parents could agree

upon it, they were charged to keep themselves chaste until the marriage is sanctified by the public prayers of the Church; for otherwise, many marriages have been punished by the Lord for the uncleanness that has been committed between the contract and the marriage.

Whether they ever were pre-contracted? Then he charged them, saying: I charge you, by authority from Jesus Christ, in whom you look to be saved, that having the consent of your parents, and having received these precepts, that (I say) you labor to grow in knowledge, and in the fear of God. And now, as in the sight of God (with all such legality as is used by others), you must make before the Lord a contract, which is far more than a promise; and it is to be done in this manner with their hands being joined. [Name] R., I promise to you, [Name] F., that I will be your husband, which I will confirm by public marriage, in pledge whereof I give you my hand. In like manner does the woman to the man. Then after the prayer, the parties are dismissed.

FINIS

Other Works Published by Puritan Publications

1647 Westminster Confession of Faith 3rd Edition – KJV Bible
A Biblical Response to Superstition, Will-Worship and the Christmas Holiday – by Daniel Cawdrey (1588-1664)
A Devotional on Our Savior's Death and Passion by Charles Herle (1598-1659)
A Discourse on Church Discipline and Reformation – by Daniel Cawdrey (1588-1664)
A Glimpse of God's Glory – Thomas Hodges (1600-1672)
A Golden Topaz, or Heart-Jewel, Namely, a Conscience Purified and Pacified by the Blood and Spirit of Christ – by Francis Whiddon (d. 1656) 2nd Ed.
A Sermon Against Lukewarmness in Religion – by Henry Wilkinson (1566-1647)
A Treatise of the Loves of Christ to His Spouse by Samuel Bolton, D.D. (1606-1654)
A Treatise on Divine Contentment – by Simeon Ashe (d. 1662)
A Vindication of the Keys of the Kingdom of Heaven into the Hands of the Right Owners – by Daniel Cawdrey (1588-1664)
Armilla Catechetica, or a Chain of Theological Principles – by John Arrowsmith (1602-1659)
Attending the Lord's Table – by Henry Tozer (1602-1650)
Christ Inviting Sinners to Come to Him for Rest – by Jeremiah Burroughs (1599-1646)
Christ the Settlement in Unsettled Times – Jeremiah Whitaker (1599–1654)
Ezra's Covenant Renewal: The Pursuit of a Lasting Reformation by Josiah Shute (1588-1643)
Family Reformation Promoted, and Other Works – by Daniel Cawdrey (1588-1664)
God is Our Refuge and Our Strength by George Gipps (n.d.)
God Paying Every Man His Due – Francis Woodcock (1614-1649)

Appendix: A Marriage Contract

God With Us, and Other Works – by John Strickland (1601-1670)
God, the Best Acquaintance of Christians – by Matthew Newcomen (1610–1669)
God's Voice from His Throne of Glory – by John Carter (d. 1655)
Gospel Peace, Or Four Useful Discourses – by Jeremiah Burroughs (1599-1646)
Gospel Worship, or, The Right Manner of Sanctifying the name of God in General, in Hearing the Word, Receiving the Lord's Supper, and Prayer by Jeremiah Burroughs (1599-1646)
Gradual Reformation Intolerable – by C. Matthew McMahon and Anthony Burgess (1600-1663)
Halting Stigmatized – by Arthur Sallaway (b. 1606)
How to Serve God in Private and Public Worship – by John Jackson (1600-1648)
Independency A Great Schism – by Daniel Cawdrey (1588-1664)
Jacob's Seed and David's Delight – by Jeremiah Burroughs (1599-1646)
Jesus Christ God's Shepherd – by William Strong (d. 1654)
Making Religion One's Business – by Herbert Palmer (1601-1647)
Presumptive Regeneration, or, the Baptismal Regeneration of Elect Infants – by Cornelius Burgess (1589-1665)
Primitive Baptism and Therein Infant's and Parent's Rights by Matthew Sylvester (1636–1708)
Real Thankfulness – by Simeon Ashe (d. 1662)
Reasonable Christianity – by Henry Hammond (1605-1660)
Reformation and Desolation – by Stephen Marshall (1594–1655)
Repentance and Fasting – by Peter Du Moulin (1601-1684) and Henry Wilkinson (1566-1647)
Rules for Our Walking With God – by Jeremiah Burroughs (1599-1646)
Salvation in a Mystery – by John Bond (1612-1676)
Scripture's Self Evidence – by Thomas Ford (1598-1674)
Selected Works of Peter Sterry – by Peter Sterry (1613-1672)
Sermons, Prayers, and Pulpit Addresses – Alexander Henderson (1583-1646)

Singing of Psalms the Duty of Christians – by Thomas Ford (1598–1674)

Spots of the Godly and of the Wicked – by Jeremiah Burroughs (1599-1646)

The All-Seeing Unseen Eye of God and Other Sermons – by Matthew Newcomen (1610–1669)

The Art of Divine Meditation by Edmund Calamy (1600-1666)

The Art of Happiness – by Francis Rous (1579–1659)

The Certainty of Heavenly and the Uncertainty of Earthly Treasures – by William Strong (d. 1654)

The Christian's Duty Towards Reformation – by Thomas Ford (1598–1674)

The Church's Need of Jesus Christ – by Thomas Valentine (1586-1665)

The Covenant of Life Opened – by Samuel Rutherford (1600-1661)

The Covenant of Works and the Covenant of Grace – by Edmund Calamy (1600-1666)

The Covenant-Avenging Sword Brandished – by John Arrowsmith (1602-1659)

The Difficulties of and Encouragements to a Reformation – Anthony Burgess (1600-1663) 2nd Ed.

The Doctrine of Man's Future Eternity – by John Jackson (1600-1648)

The Efficiency of God's Grace in Bringing Gain-Saying Sinners to Christ – by Simeon Ashe (d. 1662)

The Eternity and Certainty of Hell's Torments – by William Strong (d. 1654)

The Excellency of Holy Courage in Evil Times – by Jeremiah Burroughs (1599-1646)

The Excellent Name of God by Jeremiah Burroughs (1599-1646)

The Fall of Adam and Other Works – by John Greene (d. 1660)

The Glorious Name of God the Lord of Hosts by Jeremiah Burroughs (1599-1646)

The Glory and Beauty of God's Portion and Other Sermons – by Gaspar Hickes, (d. 1677)

Appendix: A Marriage Contract

The Godly Man's Ark – by Edmund Calamy (1600-1666)

The Growth and Spreading of Heresy – by Thomas Hodges (1600-1672)

The Guard of the Tree of Life, a Discourse on the Sacraments – by Samuel Bolton (1606-1654)

The Light of Faith and Way of Holiness – by Richard Byfield (1598–1664)

The Manifold Wisdom of God Seen in Covenant Theology – by George Walker (1581-1651)

The Nature, Danger and Cure of Temptation by Richard Capel (1586-1656)

The Necessity, Dignity and Duty of Gospel Ministers – by Thomas Hodges (1600-1672)

The Rock of Israel and Other Sermons – by Edmund Staunton (1600-1671)

The Saint's Communion with God – by William Strong, A.M. (d. 1654)

The Saint's Inheritance and the Worldling's Portion – by Jeremiah Burroughs (1599-1646)

The Saint's Will Judge the World, and Other Sermons – by Daniel Cawdrey (1588-1664)

The Sermons of William Spurstowe (1605-1666)

The Soul's Porter, or a Treatise on the Fear of God – by William Price (1597-1646)

The Spiritual Chemyst, or Divine Meditations on Several Subjects – by William Spurstowe (1605-1666)

The Sweetness of Divine Meditation by William Bridge (1600-1670)

The Trial of a Christian's Sincere Love to Christ – by William Pinke (1599–1629)

The Wells of Salvation Opened – by William Spurstowe (1605-1666)

The Worthy Churchman, or the Faithful Minister of Jesus Christ – by John Jackson (1600-1648)

The Zealous Christian – by Simeon Ashe (d. 1662)

Truth, the Great Business of Our Times – by John Maynard (1600-1665)

Zeal for God's House Quickened – by Oliver Bowles B.D. (1574-1664?)

Zion's Joy – Jeremiah Burroughs (1599-1646)

www.ingramcontent.com/pod-product-compliance
Lightning Source LLC
Chambersburg PA
CBHW030852170426
43193CB00009BA/582